To BG
Tough Guy
May God Bless

A Cowboy of a Different Kind

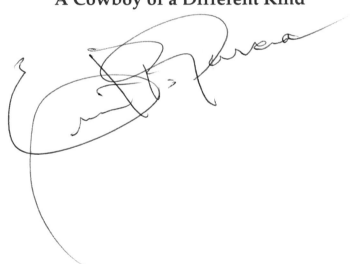

A Cowboy of a Different Kind
Memoir of a Solider

ERNEST GARCIA

Rio Rancho, New Mexico
September 2017

A Cowboy of a Different Kind
Memoir of a Man and Soldier

First edition 2017

Published by Ernest Garcia
Genre: Memoir

Includes a table of contents, glossary, and appendix

ISBN-13: 978-1545234310
ISBN-10: 1545234310

1. Memoir   2. Vietnam

Printed in the United States of America
by CreateSpace, an Amazon Company

For information about additional copies go to:
www.amazon.com

For my Mother, Lucy Byas, and Father, Felix Garcia, Sr., for bringing me into this world, and filling my life with colorful journeys. My wish as a child was to make them proud. As a man, I hope I have succeeded.

Ernest Garcia, soldier and author

Photo: Stacey Pearsal

Ernest Garcia, the youngster

Table of Contents

Preface

It was an ordinary phone call on an ordinary day. Ernest wanted to write his memoir, and I offered to meet with him to determine how much work it would be for me to edit what he had already written, augment the text, and assist him through the independent publishing process.

"Vietnam," he said. "I am a veteran and I want to write about my time in Vietnam."

* * *

That old bloody ghost—The Vietnam War—was back, speaking to me in the voice of a veteran who had seen combat.

It was the first war seen prolifically on TV. Images of civilians killed and blame for our soldiers saturated the media reports, as though they were the first troops ever to contend with hostile locals or collateral damage.

Worse, Ernest and other veterans I've worked with believe they were not allowed to win that war.

It appeared to be a conflict played out in Washington, like a game of chess. But the pieces on the board were real, breathing American youth and not inanimate wood or marble game pieces.

Looking at Vietnam soldiers' photos today, most of them were kids, fighting in a guerilla war in an intolerable climate, with a foreign threat that did not portend the death of the liberties we enjoyed in the United States.

In his post-World War II bravado regarding fending off communism anywhere in the world, President John F. Kennedy promised to "...pay any price, bear any burden, meet any hardship, support any friend...to assure the survival and success of liberty."

He decided to do it with the blood of young people. It was an inheritance from the "Greatest Generation" to its children, the baby boomer generation.

Ernest and I made an appointment to meet at a local restaurant. He warned me that although I had never met him, I would instantly recognize him.

He was right.

I looked up from the table where I was sipping some coffee to see a wiry black-haired man of medium height. He wore a weathered black leather vest bedecked with military medals, service bars, and various patches. An Army Air Cavalry hat sat firmly on his head, its golden cord hat band knotted to indicate he had been in combat. It was rather like a Stetson, complementing his rugged looks.

He pulled out a binder of material: photos, commendations, reprints of newspaper and magazine articles about him, CDs of interviews, military documents, artifacts about his current work with veterans, information about his past jobs across several industries, and a list of his combat buddies who died in Vietnam. Ernest told me he has PTSD (Post Traumatic Stress Disorder) and has received treatment. I didn't know how deeply I could delve without causing him pain or harm. So I began with some simple questions:

> What is your purpose for writing your memoir?

> Who do you think would be interested in reading it?

> What are the key ideas you want people to walk away with after they read your memoir?

> What events made the greatest impressions on you in your life, and why?

Which people have been the most influential on you, and why?

One of the first things he told me was that his wife wanted him to stop wearing his vest all the time and refrain from signaling to the world his persona was tied up in Vietnam.

"What did you say to her?" I asked.

He looked at me, tugged on each side of his vest, shrugged his shoulders, and declared, "But this is who I am!"

I let him talk, and he flooded me with a deep river of words, memories, and emotions. The current of his thoughts all led to Vietnam, as though there was nothing else in his being except the war experience. Wave after wave of specific events and people engulfed me verbally as well as in both hand-written and typed pages created as part of his PTSD therapy. I had the feeling he was drowning in recollections of Vietnam and his stories rekindled my own feelings of opposition to that war.

After we took a break to refill our coffee cups, we returned to our table and I gathered up all the Vietnam memories in a thick stack. I vowed I would take his writings and videos home, read and view them, and come up with a schedule and price for the work ahead of us. I smiled at him. "Ernest, do you know that although Vietnam was the pivotal moment in your life, you are many things in addition to being a soldier? You may have other events and relationships you may wish to include in your book."

"What do you mean?" he asked, perplexed, with squinted eyes. "Vietnam is my life."

Then I gently reminded him he is also a son, a brother, a nephew, an uncle, a husband, and a father, in addition to being a soldier and veteran. He had once been a child, and then a teenager. Now he was a grandfather. I suggested his story should cover more than his experience as a soldier and veteran...more than Vietnam.

He looked at me with a wry smile and nodded in agreement, as though he had never thought of himself as anything other than a Vietnam soldier who held a combat job that usually foisted a short life expectancy on anyone who did it.

I went home and read or viewed everything he gave me. The following week, we discussed the outline I had prepared. It ranged from his early years as a child, through his Army years, into the post war years when he fell in love and married a few times, what he sees as the legacy of war, and finally, giving back to veterans.

His memories of his childhood are warm and rich, like sweet, fresh whipped cream on warm rice pudding. As Ernest's story unfolded, I learned much about his ethnic culture, his childhood escapades, and how he and his family dealt with, and ultimately tamed poverty. His youth built the foundation for the way he handled himself in Vietnam and survived that horror, and his decision to become a soldier also said a lot about his character, as did his choice of specialty in the service. Ernest firmly believed that if his country called him to serve, then he would serve. He had no ambivalence about the values that led him to enlist, even if he had misgivings about the particular war that dominated his generation.

As I worked with Ernest, I came to understand the extent to which he believed the military helped him become a man and we remembered how many Americans succumbed to hating soldiers returning from Vietnam. It is almost as though the servicemen and servicewomen who had served in Southeast Asia were never really wanted back home. When Ernest spoke of the way the media portrayed Vietnam soldiers, I could see the anger and pain were still raw almost fifty years later.

It occurred to me that as Americans, we appreciate our latest crop of veterans more deeply today. Perhaps that is because, if only for a brief moment, everyone understood we faced existential threats to our way of life on September 11, 2001. Yet, I suspect it is something more.

Consider how our gratitude for today's newest veterans contrasts so sharply with the callousness Vietnam veterans experienced. They were often reviled by many. As a nation, are we overcompensating for past sins of omission? We ignored the needs of Vietnam vets, failed to consider them warriors working on our behalf, and regarded them, thanks to Hollywood and the media, as hopeless drug-addicted miscreants. If seems we deserve the penance of guilt.

Ernest's book is complete. His memoir defines him as a man with a life both before and after Vietnam, but he is a man whose identity is inextricably woven into the web of pain and confusion of the war. He is a man who knows his place in history, did his share for our country when asked, suffered for it, and lives a successful, fulfilling life, nonetheless.

It is he, and not some hollow sports or entertainment figure, who is a true hero. Welcome home, solider.

Patricia Walkow
Author, *The War Within, the Story of Josef*

September 2017

The Family Home

This is a photo of the family home on 17th Street in McAllen, Texas, where the Gonzalez family grew up.

Photo courtesy Ernest Garcia

Introduction

I am from Texas, and Texas draws images of cowboys and horses. So many times, I have been asked if I am a cowboy. In a way, I am. Not the typical kind, though, riding a horse on the range, guarding and driving cattle. Instead, I was in the Army. In Vietnam, I flew with the 3/17th Air Cav, 1st Infantry Division and the 3/5th Air Cav, 9th Infantry Division.

As a member of a Cavalry unit, I paid tribute to the olden days, when soldiers rode horses. Unlike the cavalry of the past who galloped across the earth on steeds made of flesh and blood and hair, our horses were made of metal and wire and flew above the treetops. I rode helicopters with 1400 shaft horsepower, and not on the open ranges of the American West, but above Vietnam, Laos, and Cambodia, looking for the enemy—the Viet Cong. My fellow combat soldiers and I wore cavalry hats that looked a little like cowboy hats, but with a crossed sword emblem.

Although my years in Vietnam comprise a momentous time in my life, my childhood, as well as the years after Vietnam, also contributed greatly to who I am today—a man from the barrios of McAllen, Texas who had an upbringing rich in love, if not money. I am a man who served his country, held interesting jobs, met fascinating people, and loved a few special women. Today, I devote my life to helping veterans. A wise man I knew, Chief Warrant Officer Don Callison of the 3/5th Air Cav once said, "If we are not willing to record our own history, we shouldn't complain when some stranger gets it wrong."

This is my story, my history for all to read...stranger, friend, and family. It is the story of a cowboy of a different kind.

Ernest Garcia, September 2017

Hidalgo County, Texas

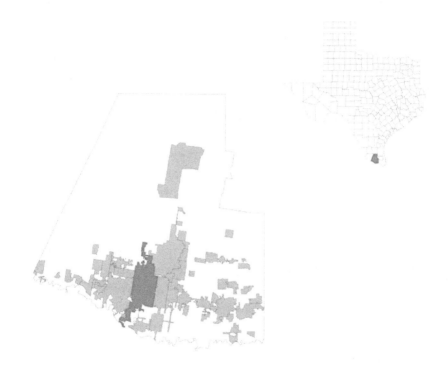

Map of South Texas - McAllen

Map courtesy Create Commons, Wikipedia, State of Texas

Chapter 1: The Early Years

Memories of when I was a child make me feel blessed. Although I can't turn back the hands of time, I will always recall the moments and events of life in the *barrio*, with my family and friends. Through the years, I have come to realize it's not the neighborhood you live in that counts; it's the neighbor you are.

I was born in St. Louis, Missouri in 1950, where my father worked at McDonnell Douglas Aircraft as a sheet metal worker. When that job ended, we moved to McAllen, Texas, where I grew up. I was four years old at the time. My mother told me that when we got to McAllen, I had shoulder-length golden brown hair, but the kids in the barrio would have none of it, and they would sometimes throw rocks at me. It was not long before I got a dignified haircut.

All of us were poor. We had to be creative and improvise in order to increase our household incomes. As kids, my siblings and I seemed to possess an innate ability to enjoy life, which was uncomplicated. My four brothers, two sisters, and I filled the house. I was the second oldest child.

Our barrio was a united group of neighbors and we helped each other. Even though we had the *Pacucos* families in our neighborhood, with their starched, baggy khaki pants and spit-shined shoes, they were never a problem because they kept the riff-raff out. These local thugs were a rough breed, but they always protected their turf. It was like they were our Robin Hoods, ready to give back to the barrio, and khaki pants became very popular in our corner of the world.

I recall when my family was the only one that had a television. Dad had managed to come up with one, and it was even before we had indoor plumbing. The neighborhood—family and friends—would gather at our house to watch the baseball games and wrestling matches. Although we had only a

1½ bedroom house, we always managed to accommodate everyone, despite their needing to sit on the cement floor. For us, there was no such thing as carpeting in those days. Yet, through the television, wrestlers Fritz Von Eric, Kinchi Chaboya, and others became our heroes. Our town certainly loved youth baseball games, and it seemed every kid I knew was involved in Pee Wee League, Little League, Farm League, or Pony League. Neighborhoods would shut down when there was a game because everybody was at the ball park. My brother Felix, our cousins, and friends were very involved with baseball. Our parents could not always afford to buy us uniforms, but sometimes we found a company to sponsor us and outfit our team. I fondly remember the exhilarating feeling of putting on the team uniform. It made me feel very tall and proud. We would pretend we were in the major leagues, and would imitate our baseball favorites. There were a lot of favorites: Hank Aaron, Carlos Beltran, Johnny Bench, Jose Bautista, Roger Clemens, Joe Dimaggio, Don Drysdale, Whitey Ford, Ken Griffey, Mickey Mantle, Jose Iglesias, Pee Wee Reese, Nolan Ryan, Matt Holliday, and more.

We also collected many baseball cards and comic books. The baseball cards came with a thin sheet of pink bubble gum. The comic books, baseball cards, and bubble gum kept us kids off the streets and out of trouble.

We would subsidize our ability to buy trading cards and school supplies by raiding agricultural fields full of citrus fruit, carrots, onions, melons, corn, lettuce, turnips, beets, cauliflower, grapes, beans, soybeans, cotton, sugar cane, and the famous Sweet Texas 1015 onions. We'd fill our Little Red Arrow wagons with fruits and vegetables, selling them door-to-door to the Gringos who lived on the other side of the irrigation canal. Proceeds of our sales grew quickly from our stash of freshly-picked and stolen goods. Our parents appreciated the extra incomes when times were hard. My father, brothers, and I sometimes picked cotton for two cents a pound.

Bugler brand tobacco sold for twelve cents a pack. Dad would send me to the corner store, Rivas Food Market, to purchase it, and he would wait for me to return home, his cigarette-rolling machine on hand and ready for him to operate it.

Mom worked at Rexall Drugs in the cosmetics department. It was a mom and pop type of store, with a lunch counter. You could get the best hamburger in town there, not to mention malteds, shakes, and banana splits. On her time off, Mom would make stacks of fresh tortillas when we had the funds to purchase 100-pound sacks of flour and 50-pound cans of lard. I smile when I recall the scent of the warm tortillas, and Mom would always find a way to have apple butter to spread on them as they came off, fresh, from the *comal*.

When I was somewhere between eight and ten years old, I started having trouble reading. My eyesight wasn't good, and I got my first pair of glasses through the Lions Club, through a Dr. Beardsley, the optometrist who worked with the Lions Club.

My uncle, George Salinas, was the chief criminal investigator for the McAllen, Texas Police Department. He was stern, yet caring, and worked his way up through the ranks. He commanded respect and the bad *hombres* were wary of him. While he was in his patrol car and met up with my little clique of friends, he would pull up to us and ask, "What are you *banditos* up to now? Why aren't you at home?"

We always acted innocent, but I never stopped reminding my friends that he was my uncle.

Usually we would go all over town, either by walking or riding our bicycles. Once we were old enough—I'd say somewhere between twelve and fourteen—and interested enough, we would scour our town for girls, or look for ways to make a few bucks, and often hang out in the railroad cars waiting on the tracks along the canal. They would stand idly by, ready to move along a row of packing sheds where processed fruits and vegetables would be loaded, and then transported to markets near and far. Of course, one of biggest thrills was to

3

walk, or run, and then jump from car to car, as the train moved. That was after we climbed on top of them, and it was sometimes a challenge to jump from one railroad car to the next. When the cars were stationary, the doors were always open, and we would sneak inside one of the cars to use it as our hangout.

Simple pleasures.

Great fun, too, especially when we would go to the Rivas store and shoplift school supplies. Afterwards, we would meet in our hideout boxcar and split our take. So we were hardly ever in need of school supplies at the start of each school year. Our parents never could understand why they didn't have to worry about buying us anything for school. My thieving buddies and I called ourselves *La ganga* and I would tell my mother, "Mom, don't worry, the Lions Club and others donate to our elementary school."

My grandmother on my father's side was wonderful, a joy, and a pioneer. She worked in the fields, and would travel to California each summer to work the farms there. She was a widow, and did what she had to do to make ends meet. I can still picture her in my mind. She had one tooth—the upper front, but she was loved by all who knew her. Whenever we stopped by her one-bedroom, wooden home, she would have Kool Aid for us. The only drawback was that she had to use cheesecloth to strain the Kool Aid because of the summer infestation of tiny ants. In our part of Texas, extremely high temperatures and humidity made the ants thrive. The sugar sack was also usually full of them.

There were no swimming pools open to the public. Once in a while, we managed to sneak into a motel pool. Sometimes, we resorted to swimming in the murky waters of the irrigation canals, and we also learned how to fish there. Normally, we would catch perch or rainbow carp. Applying Mexican ingenuity, we fished with safety pins and apple cores, since we couldn't afford to buy official fishing hooks or bait. We adapted, and made do with whatever we had, and still felt blessed.

4

One street away from my house there lived a lady who had turned her home into a candy store. She had built-in sliding glass windows from which she sold all sorts of sweets to those of us who lined up to purchase them. Even snow cones. She kept the neighborhood children supplied with all kinds of treats, whether they coast a penny, a nickel, or a dime...we would buy whatever we could afford.

We collected Indian head dimes which are very had to find today. Now and then, we would lay shiny pennies on the railroad tracks, just for the excitement of seeing the train run over and flatten them. Then we compared the shapes of each flattened copper penny. Simple pleasures...great fun.

There was a vacant lot at the corner of our street. Sometimes we used it to play baseball or war games. We created our own weapons with broom handles, strips of tire tubing, and clothes pins. I used green China berries as bullets. We were ingenious. Our friend, Pepe Ballesteros, my brother Felix, and cousins Faustino and Mike Garcia would create the wildest schemes to keep us entertained. We made our own fun, our own world, and at night we might just lay there, look up at the heavens, enjoy the night stars, and imagine worlds far away. We would find the Big Dipper or Little Dipper and other constellations, and try to imagine the shapes of animals.

It was peaceful, a simple pleasure.

Felix and I had a newspaper route when we were somewhere between ten and twelve years old. At about 4:00 a.m., *The Monitor* would drop our load of newspapers at our house. We rolled them and secured each newspaper with a rubber band. We loaded them into our dual saddle back pouches, and secured the pouches to our bicycles.

Through the early morning darkness, and often chased by dogs, we whisked through our quiet neighborhood, throwing papers on driveways and front walks. Those hours were perfect for our work, before the blazing sun and humidity of south Texas could take its toll on us.

On September 5th, 1967, Hurricane Beulah paid us a visit from the Gulf of Mexico. In its wake were miles and miles of massive flooding and destruction on both sides of the Rio Grande. Between McAllen and Hidalgo, Texas, levees were manned by National Guard troops and civilian volunteers filling sandbags to help prevent more flooding. For several days, everybody and his brother and sister headed to the levees to lend a hand. We didn't complain, nor did we give it a second thought. We just wanted to protect our town and our country, convinced that just one more sandbag would save our land from Beulah, the enemy. We worked as patriots.

From grade school through high school, despite our being Hispanic kids from the barrio, we were taught to appreciate America and its freedom. My father and my uncles fought in the Korean War. They were veterans. Our devotion to our country became second nature to us. We were raised to love our country, take care of it, and love the flag.

Despite patriotism, one time my father got involved in a cantina brawl at a local pub. Mom got so mad at him for going out, drinking. Dad came home from the pub, and he and Mom got into a big argument. She sent me across the street to my uncle's house to call the police. We could not afford a phone.

The police cars showed up and tried to diffuse the situation with the help of my uncle, the criminal investigator. My Dad was so angry that it took three policemen to subdue and handcuff him. He was so powerful, he broke through three sets of cuffs. With the fourth set of cuffs, the police finally got him under control and placed him in the back seat of the squad car, but they managed to slam the door and shut it on his thumb. Although it was an accident, slamming the door on his thumb helped to subdue him. Until the day he died, Dad bore a black thumbnail, testifying to his earlier days of battle. I was proud of my Dad, of his strength and resistance. Who else can say his Dad broke three pairs of handcuffs before the entire neighborhood? People in the barrio still talk about it. Yet, he was a quiet and gentle giant to me, and is my hero. I was awarded a Bronze Star in the Army, and I dedicated it to him.

* * *

Everyone is human, though, and my Mom and Dad married and divorced two or three times. I lost count, but my love for my Dad has always stood out, and I was his favorite, I believe.

He had broad shoulders, and my mother always bragged about them. His chest was wide and I always felt sheltered in his arms. He seemed indestructible to me, and I would be happy to be half the man he was. His impact on me was enormous.

My Mom raised seven children. While we lived in poverty, she told anyone who would listen that I contributed ¾ of my paycheck to the household, even when I made only thirty-five to fifty cents an hour. I worked at the grocery store my grandfather, Ismael Gonzalez, Sr., owned. Mom was tenacious in finding ways to feed and clothe us, being sure we were never without the necessities. She was a single parent for the most part, and learned how to deal effectively with the welfare system. A real fighter. And still a fighter, at 89 years old. She continues to live in McAllen and never learned to drive. She walks to the store, to the mall, and everywhere. It's exercise for her, and she enjoys her private time and window shopping along the way to her various destinations. Mom has always been passionate about style, and, despite her lack of a lot of money, the people in the old neighborhood still remember her as their very own "Best Dressed Woman."

She still gets all dolled-up from head to toe when she goes out, right up to her false eyelashes.

Four Little Garcias Playing by the Stream

Carefree days playing along the banks of the Guadalupe River near the house where Ernest's father lived, in Kerrville, Texas. It was in the hill country. From the left: Ernest, Linda, Felix Jr., and Cynthia.

Photo courtesy Ernest Garcia

Jeffrey Lynn and Ernest Garcia

Brothers Jeffrey Lynn (left) and Ernest posing on a Mustang. Esmer's photo (Esmer was Ernest's girlfriend at the time) is perched on the car.

Photo courtesy Ernest Garcia

Uncle Ismael Gonzalez, Jr. Outside his Store

Photo courtesy Ernest Garcia

Grocery Store Owned by Ernest's Grandfather, Ismael Gonzalez, Sr.

Photo Courtesy Ernest Garcia

Wedding Day: Ernest's Parents, Felix Sr., and Lucilla

Photo Courtesy Ernest Garcia

Chapter 2: Becoming a Soldier

I wish my father was still alive to witness and be proud of me and my accomplishments in life, especially my life in the Army. I joined to follow in his footsteps.

I had dropped out of high school to work and subsidize our household income. My Mom was afraid of my joining the military, having already lost a son, Jeffrey Lynn, to cancer when he was just seventeen.

My first thought was to find security from serving in Vietnam so as not to worry my family more than necessary.

The military recruiting officers were in the Federal Building in McAllen. Since I had many options for service, I decided to explore the Navy, first. As I walked into the Navy Recruiting Office on May 5, 1969, the recruiter on duty asked how he could help me.

"I want to see what the Navy has to offer me," I replied.

He sternly answered back, "No, it's what do *you* have to offer the navy!" in a sarcastic tone of voice.

"With your attitude, I don't need your damn Navy," I informed him. "Thank you very much!"

Two minutes later I was at the Army Recruiting Office, signing up.

The Army guaranteed me the schooling I wanted. Looking to better myself, I wanted to learn an occupation that could serve me well in the future. I qualified for Avionics Tech school and embraced it. My formal training was in the Signal Corp at Fort Gordon, Georgia. When basic training ended I took a leave, and when I returned, reported for MOS (Military Occupational Specialty) 35K20 training, to become a specialist in avionics.

An avionics specialist performs maintenance on tactical communications, flight control, and navigation equipment. Avionic techs learned to perform maintenance checks on flight controls, stabilize systems such as SCAS (Stability and Control Augmentation Systems), and controlled encryption technology for the AH-1G Huey Cobra Gunships, which were helicopters. In addition, they learned how to diagnose problems, troubleshoot any issues that arose, and maintain both ordinary and specialized tools, as well as keep the maintenance shop stocked with all the proper gear.

First, though, came ten weeks of basic combat training when we learned how to fight. It was intense. We ran a lot—from the mess hall, and in the field. We learned how to clean and use weapons and engage in combat. Reveille was at 5 a.m., and physical fitness exercises honed me from a 115-pound weakling to 135 pounds of muscle.

It was as though parts of me were placed in a machine, and out came a soldier fit for combat.

I was proud to wear the uniform. The discipline helped me become a man, and prepared me to perform the work of a man.

After basic training, I engaged in twenty-four weeks of advanced individual training, with both classroom and on-the-job training in avionics. I had to study basic electronic theory, learn soldering, systems installation practices, and restoration of avionics systems and sub systems.

I became proficient with automatic direction finders (ADF), including transponders and GPS (global positioning systems), VOR (Very High Frequency omni-directional radio range), and LOC (Localizer). I mastered receivers, indicators, antennae, speakers, and audio address amplifiers and controls, as well as different kinds of frequencies: HF, VHF, and UHF.

Those of us in the training program also learned to handle VOR, ILS, Glidescope marker beacon and navigation receivers and controls. We handled transponders, RADAR, X Band RADAR, C Band RADAR, and altimeters, VFW Comm, DME, and VOR/LOC.

Fortunately, I was an Army volunteer, and not a draftee, so my avionics training was part of my enlistment contract.

Towards the end of my avionics training, I had the option to sign up for an advanced program, because my grades were high enough. I was selected for the course of study and was automatically promoted to a SP/4 (Specialist 4). The program was created to fill the need for non-commissioned officers in Vietnam...people who had avionics skills. Once I graduated from the advanced program, I was promoted to SP/5, (Specialist 5) and part of the instruction was conducted in a mock-up setting of Vietnam. But that SP/5 designation and graduation from advanced training pretty much guaranteed I would be sent to Vietnam.

Within eleven months of joining the Army, I jumped from E-1 to E-5 (SP/5), which was a major milestone for me. By then, I knew my critical MOS was urgently needed in the war zone. I quickly obtained a top security clearance which would allow me to work with critical radio systems in the Army's helicopters.

My training completed, I was given orders to ship to Vietnam.

Reality started to set in, knowing I would soon be deployed to a war zone.

* * *

Deployments are easier when the nation recognizes a need.

Few questioned the necessity of engagement during World War II, or even Korea. Vietnam was different, however, a war seen on television, unlike previous wars.

At first, the conflict was considered vital to stemming the advancement of communism.

As military casualties mounted and American citizens saw on the nightly news the searing images of wounded soldiers and South Vietnamese citizens, the motives for the war seemed to become murky. Many in the U.S. turned against our engagement in Southeast Asia, and to a certain extent, the soldiers who fought the war.

This was the environment in which I headed to Vietnam.

But, prior to my going overseas, I was on leave for thirty days and I went home to visit my family and friends, and my girlfriend, Esmer—short for Esmeralda.

Thirty days can seem like a long time, but it really isn't.

As the end of my leave approached, I often thought about what my life in Vietnam would be like. I was apprehensive, but I felt I was well-trained to do my job and could meet any challenge.

I had an attitude of "Let's do this thing" and it helped me cope with my anxieties.

On the day I was to deploy, my family accompanied me to the airport. My father couldn't be there, because he was no longer living in McAllen at the time.

I tried to be strong and not show any fear, especially for my mother and Esmer, whose brother—my best friend, Jimmy Herrera, a Marine—was already in the war zone. Esmer was frightened for me, and my mother was in tears. Before I left, Esmer handed me a small tape recorder so I could "talk" to her and she could hear my voice when I sent the tape back to her.

It was October of 1970. Standing on the tarmac, I was trying to be brave for my girlfriend, my family, and myself. I knew there was no turning back, and I offered a silent prayer, "Please help me become a man for my country."

That day, waiting to board the airplane, I left behind the people I loved, my childhood, and all that was familiar.

My next experience would be war. Vietnam.

* * *

Getting to Southeast Asia took about two days.

We flew first from McAllen to Oakland, California, then on to Anchorage, Alaska. From there we flew to Guam, but we only refueled there. Among all the palm trees I was struck by the poverty of the people and settlements I could see. From Guam we flew to Japan, and had a beautiful view of Mt. Fuji.

Finally, we landed in Saigon.

I had arrived in Vietnam. Now, I was part of the war.

Locations in Vietnam

In the public domain, from George L. MacGarrigle, The United States Army in Vietnam: Combat Operations, Taking Offensive, October 1966-October 1967. Washington DC: Center of Military History, 1998.

Chapter 3: Vietnam

Some background about our country's engagement in Vietnam might be in order.

In 1961, President John F. Kennedy agreed to finance the expansion of the South Vietnamese army, in order to bolster its efforts to fight the communist threat from the North. This was an extension of President Dwight D. Eisenhower's support for the South Vietnamese government which was already in effect when Kennedy took office.

President Kennedy was a champion of freedom and stated that the United States would "...pay any price, bear any burden, meet any hardship, support any friend...to assure survival and success of liberty."

After Kennedy was assassinated in 1963, Lyndon Johnson served the remainder of slain president's term and then became a candidate in his own right, running on a platform of peace and prosperity and increased social welfare benefits for certain segments of the American population. He easily defeated candidate Barry Goldwater who was not as generous with taxpayer's money and was considered somewhat of a hawk, regarding war.

Regardless, the conflict in Vietnam escalated. In 1965, to satisfy the requirements of the ever-expanding American military effort in Vietnam, the "peace and prosperity" President activated the Selective Service System, mailing military induction notices to young men. These little greetings accelerated at a rapid pace; the draft was back.

Operating through a network of around 3,700 local draft boards, Selective Service mailed 13,700 notices in April of 1965, and another 15,100 in May. In July, the number climbed to 27,400 and by December it was over 40,000.

It had been only twenty years since the end of World War II in 1945 and twelve years since the end of U.S. combat engagement in South Korea in 1953. Protests mounted. Mass demonstrations were staged by students and peace groups. Draft cards were burned, sit-ins were staged, and local draft boards were targeted for vandalism. But I remembered the inspiring words of John F. Kennedy during his inaugural speech and took it to heart. "Ask not what your country can do for you, but what you can do for your country."

Heeding his call, I enlisted, and was sent to Vietnam.

* * *

When our plane arrived in Saigon, we immediately received immunizations for diseases like cholera, among others. Then we were issued infantry fatigues and gear. The air was thick with humidity, and it was hot. Fortunately, I was used to moisture-saturated air and heat, although it seemed worse in Vietnam.

Once we were processed, we were placed on buses for the trip to our base at Dĩ An where my unit, the 1st Aviation Brigade 3/17 Air Cav, was based. It was dark during the bus trip as we headed into the unknown, unaware of anything around us. We were all on edge.

Weary from the long journey, we settled into our hooches—that's what we called our living quarters—for the night. Our accommodations were lined all around on the outside with sandbags to dampen the effects of any grenades or gunshots. I had not yet been assigned a weapon.

During that first night, I was bolted awake.

We were under attack. Machine gun fire and mortars were hurled at us. I was beyond terrified, and one of my hooch mates made sure I stayed low, and he covered for me, since I had no weapon. Somehow, I had the foresight to turn on the tape recorder to capture the sounds of the battle. I sent it to Esmer, but over the years, it got lost.

20

Maybe that's for the best.

After the attack stopped, we assessed the damage to our camp, tended to the wounded, and identified our fallen comrades who died.

So ended my first night in Vietnam.

The next morning, the base returned to business as usual, and that was the pattern followed after any encounter with the enemy, despite the dead or wounded from the previous day.

* * *

I quickly became the NCO (Non-Commissioned Officer) in charge of the avionics shop.

One of my duties was to prepare daily reports to the CO (Commanding Officer). These reports identified the status of damaged (red-x) helicopters that were no longer flight-worthy, usually due to extensive small arms fire damage from the enemy—the North Vietnamese Army (NVA) and the Viet Cong. Fortunately, I was soon assigned to a 2nd Lieutenant who, as my superior officer, took on the responsibility of producing the daily reports, leaving me free to do the actual avionics work.

My CO had a degree in electronics, and was usually a pain in my side. I had become a seasoned avionics specialist and knew how to diagnose problems and solve them.

This new 2nd Lieutenant believed he was always correct when he had to analyze problems with equipment. He had the degree and rank, but I had much more experience than he did, and one day I had heard enough of his theories and decided to put him in his place. I stopped him in mid-sentence to state what was on my mind.

"Sir," I said, "please forgive me for saying this, but you are so smart you are actually dumb."

Fortunately, he was in a good mood, despite the fact his head snapped to attention and jaw fell open at my comment. He could have court-martialed me, but to my surprise, he agreed. We both had a good laugh over it, even though I knew I was taking a big gamble by saying what I did to him.

Ernest as a Young Avionics Specialist in Vietnam

Photo courtesy Ernest Garcia

I taught him a lot of practical things, but he was excellent with mathematics and engineering. One of his brainstorms was to mount a PRC25, a common field radio used in the war, on the underbelly of a Huey helicopter so the pilots could have direct communications with the ground troops, eliminating the need to have to go through headquarters while flying to, through, and from hostile landing zones. It was quite successful.

* * *

We had thirty-five choppers assigned to us: Cobra gunships, bubble-cabin Loaches, Kiowas, and Hueys. Each one was in dire need of repair of some kind. Only my new CO and I had the authority to red-x a helicopter. Not even the Company CO could override us.

My CO, my assistant, and I often worked long days, ranging from twelve to as many as eighteen hours, in the extreme heat. Our work was a priority to the Company Commander. Without all systems GO, with full communications and navigation equipment functioning, we might jeopardize the crew of a mission. Combat missions were dangerous enough, and our avionics work helped ensure our pilots, crew chiefs, door gunners, and light infantry squads would fly safely.

Inside a helicopter there are various wire bundles, some with up to fifty wires going out of a male connector feeding a female connector throughout the length of the chopper. Maybe it was Murphy's law, or maybe it was just the nature of combat, but there were always about eight to ten helicopters needing repair due to small arms fire finding its way to one of the wire bundles.

Sometimes, rewiring something like a tailboom had to be done from the underside of the chopper, where it was necessary to remove a panel with fifty or so screws, and we had to squirm and squeeze our bodies inside to work. We worked in constant heat and humidity. I arrived in Vietnam weighting 150 pounds, and left weighing 135 pounds. I lost fifteen pounds of sweat there.

Photo at Quảng Trị

Ernest Garcia, left, with Eloy Martinez. Quảng Trị combat base. Notice the sandbags at the base of the huts, placed there to offer some protection from mortar fire and hand grenades lobbed by the enemy.

Photo courtesy Ernest Garcia

Air Cavalry Hat

Ernest's Air Cavalry hat indicates he was in combat, as demonstrated by the gold cord that is knotted on each side of the center cylinder, beneath his bronze star.

Photo by Patricia Walkow

As time went on, I offered my services as a door gunner. In my book, *Door Gunner*, I detail my transformation from serving in Vietnam as an avionics specialist working sixteen hours a day, to a helicopter door gunner who shot at the enemy below from the open door of a chopper. Although I volunteered to take on this additional role, it is still a mystery to me how I found time to fly when I was so busy seven days a week keeping our helicopters flight-ready. The workload was great enough that it seemed as though every day was Monday. Fortunately, my assistant and my CO could do some of the work in my absence when I was in the air shooting at the enemy.

* * *

It was often said the life of a door gunner might be less than thirty minutes when in combat, if it was a bad day.

My index fingers became my best friends. To this date, I still study them and realize the power they had when I sat at the open door of my Huey or Kiowa, manning my M-60, M-16, or .45 caliber armaments, firing away for the kill. It was easy pickings, flying at treetop level and firing out into the open at twenty or thirty Viet Cong at a time. To get them to make themselves visible and vacate their hiding places, we would drop phosphorous grenades, called "Willy Petes" into the openings of tunnels. It forced them to run out, screaming in pain as their skin burned. That's when we mowed down our adversaries with our bullets. It was war. As a gunner, the adrenaline would shoot through me to the point where I could not control the shaking in my legs. It was either them or us, and certainly, they would not afford us any mercy if the tables were turned.

Just ask any prisoner of war who survived incarceration.

On another separate mission, which I was not involved in, headquarters received a radio report from a pilot about five enemy troops who were spotted in a bomb crater.

A Door Gunner, Vietnam War

A bungee cord secures the Vietnam War soldier's M-60 machine gun to the doorway of the helicopter.

The enemy scrambled and fired at our helicopter, and the door gunner and crew chief opened fire with all they had, including grenades.

When the shooting stopped and the crew landed, the body count over the radio was reported at "4½ bodies." It was a bloody mess, and half of one body could not be accounted for at all. It was also the first time the dead soldiers were reported as Chinese, not Vietnamese, and it provided proof the enemy was being supported by China.

* * *

In combat, buddies are as close as brothers. They share an unbreakable bond. Out of all the missions I flew during the heat of war, I lost track of how many times I had to place my buddies' shot, mangled, and burned bodies in body bags. Their remains were transported back to base for a memorial service before their final flight home. I wanted to fly home vertically—alive—not in a flag-draped coffin. But nothing could allay my guilt for being still alive. When I had time to tally it all up, I realized in the one year I served in the war zone, I lost forty fellow soldiers. They were men I knew and worked with. Buddies. Comrades.

These honored dead were my classmates, pilots, co-pilots, crew chiefs, door gunners, and light infantry squad members. I flew with them and worked with them in avionics in the III Corp, Cambodia, Khe Sahn, Laos, and I Corp. Among them is one of my friends, Jackie Ray Brooks. He committed suicide in front of us, playing Russian roulette, after he had received a "Dear John" letter from his wife back home.

My hatred of the enemy grew every day.

I would go out on a chopper any chance I could get. It was how I earned my flight wings and Bronze Star, but I would trade all that to get my friends back.

A current friend of mine, Michael Miller, is a fellow cast member of the *Telling, Albuquerque Project*, where several of us who had been in the military or were part of a military family tell our stories. Conducted in a theatre, it is designed to deepen the audience's understanding of the lives of veterans and other members of the military, including spouses and children.

Michael said something that is so true: "War just changes you, whether you're carrying a weapon or not. Being present in it will change you. You see things nobody should ever have to see, and some people have to do things that no one should do."

Michael was referring to me and all combat soldiers.

I often wonder why the Army did not give us erasers upon leaving Vietnam, to help us forget.

But you can't forget.

* * *

My unit, which had originally been stationed at Dĩ An, moved to Quảng Trị and used Khe San as a field base for work in the tri-border area—a no man's land of South Vietnam, North Vietnam, and Laos. We were allowed to shoot at anything that moved, walked, or talked. This area appeared to be the infiltration routes of the NVA for moving troops, equipment, and armaments to South Vietnam.

On one particularly memorable rescue mission, a pilot and I were dropped onto a landing zone to try to extract a downed chopper. The pilot had radioed that the helicopter might be flyable. We did manage to start and fly the aircraft, but as we started receiving fire, we took quite a few hits, and lost both power and hydraulic fluid. We had to auto rotate and we crash-landed, missing a river by just a few feet.

My knees slammed into the console, but there wasn't a moment for either pain or complaining. The NVA kept coming towards us for the kill, but the pilot keyed his mic and instructed me to bail out to the right, while he would go left and find cover.

The pilot carried a handgun, a 38 special, in his shoulder holster, but I handed him my M-16 machine gun nonetheless. I had my M-60 with a partial belt of ammo approximately two feet long, as well as my 45-caliber handgun. As soon as we were out of the chopper and found some safety about thirty yards from our disabled helicopter, we opened fire on the enemy.

Meanwhile, our Cobra gunships and Hueys were right above us, providing suppressive cover at the NVA. There were about thirty or forty of the enemy, and all hell broke loose with so much fire power. It seemed like an eternity, and while two COBRAS were taking care of business, two Hueys came in to pull us out of there. All of us were still under fire from the NVA.

One Huey came in from the right, and the other from the left of the downed helicopter, while we ran to them. The crew chiefs and door gunners fired their M-60s non-stop over our heads.

I ran to one of them, and the pilot to the other. The Huey I ran to had a crew chief who was one my best buddies, James, from Somerset, Texas. He stopped shooting for a few seconds while he extended his right arm to me. As my right leg stepped on the chopper's skid, he pulled me in and pushed me behind him on his canvas seat, then commenced firing once again. The Huey flew backwards, turned right, and gained altitude.

Headquarters ordered the Cobra pilots to destroy the downed chopper the pilot and I had tried to get flying again. No one wanted the gooks (that's what we called those fighting us) to obtain any radio systems and flight logs, or ammo. The location was considered a hot landing zone, and we weren't going to take any chances trying to retrieve the aircraft again. It became collateral damage.

As we gained altitude, I sat up, and James hollered at me, "Dammit Tex, how many times have I told you to stay out of the trees?" In combat, helicopters often flew just above the trees, and "staying out of the trees" meant "don't get shot down." We both laughed our way back to base at Khe Sanh. The best part, though, was that we all made it out of the firefight and didn't have to contend with any memorial services. The next day, it was back to work, as normal, as though nothing had happened.

My CO chewed me out for getting myself into such a bad situation. However, he didn't do it in a nasty way, mostly, I think, because he knew that I would always be on the first available chopper that needed a door gunner.

Looking back after all these years, I suspect that was when he nominated me for a Bronze Star.

* * *

My interactions with the South Vietnamese were limited. Civilians were allowed to work on base, and I had a hooch maid who washed my clothing and bedding and kept my quarters clean. When she washed my fatigues, it took hours for them to dry due to the humidity. Most of the time, I had no choice but to wear those uniforms, even though they were still damp and smelled musty.

I don't remember my maid's name, but I do recall she was about nineteen or twenty years old, and beautiful. We would try to communicate as best as we could, but neither of us made an attempt at any conversations of a personal nature. But I did enjoy teasing her. She was so cute, but we maintained a level of respect between us.

There were some good times despite the war, the heat, and the humidity. Our unit had a jeep we all loved to drive. "Appaloosa" was what we named it. Sometimes, we towed a little trailer behind it, filled with ice and beer.

Twice during the year, at the wind-down of some major activity, we had a celebration. When the beer was disappearing and the ice was melting, we NCOs would grab and carry the company CO and every pilot and throw them into the ice water. It was a blast...at least for us.

I enjoyed my nicknames. One was "Tex" and my radio call sign was "Roving Gypsy" and we would invent some amusing phrases when I talked to the tower pilots: "This is Roving Gypsy Fox Mike COMO check. How copy?" Some would respond back with "Got you Lima Charlie or Lumpy Chicken for "loud and clear." The whole idea of using our private lingo was to confuse the enemy who might be listening in to our conversations.

Sometimes, while flying missions just above the trees, we would pass over a village. The inhabitants had outdoor shower areas, without roofs. From time to time, we could see a female or two taking a shower and would shamelessly hover overhead. As GIs, we hadn't seen the beauty of a naked woman for months and months, and seeing them was heavenly, although I can imagine they did not think so.

At our post in Quảng Trị, just a few miles from the Demilitarized Zone (DMZ) between North and South Vietnam, we sometimes would enjoy a USO concert. On one occasion, country singer Roy Acuff was the headliner, and he brought with him an entourage of about a half dozen, incredibly beautiful American women. It had been months since most of us had seen an American woman, and those GIs who were on their 2nd or 3rd tour of duty hadn't seen one in years. If the enemy didn't kills us, the good looks of those gals could come close to doing it!

During my tour in Vietnam, showman Bob Hope was scheduled to give a performance at our base in Dĩ An. The fact such a headliner would be entertaining us uplifted everyone's spirits. Then the unthinkable happened. The selection process for who would attend the performance excluded we veteran troops who had dirty fatigues and faded combat boots. It seemed the "newbies"—recent arrivals in Vietnam—with their un-faded fatigues and shiny boots were selected to present a clean image to the world that played down the reality of life in a combat zone to those at home watching on television, appeasing the growing anti-war movement. To say those of us who just came off a combat mission felt betrayed would be a huge understatement. That episode was just an inkling of the indifference and even hatred many Vietnam vets would experience back in the States in the coming years.

One time, all grubby and wearing the visible signs of combat in a jungle, my buddies and I flew into Da Nang from Quảng Trị.

Da Nang was a huge base and we landed in the flight line. We did not dare leave our weapons inside our Huey because scavengers could, and would strip the chopper for anything of value, including the avionics parts.

We were hungry and wanted a satisfying meal and were directed to a PX-type building with a mess hall that was enormous. To protect them from being stolen, we carried all of our weapons with us. We door gunners and our crew chief walked into the dining hall with our M-60s on our shoulders, and the pilots also wore their flight gear and weapons. Talk about looking and feeling like Rambo! Every GI in the mess hall froze when they saw us walking into their immaculate dining room. They wore starched, spotless fatigues and spit-shined boots. We had mud, dirt, and sweat all over us. It made me wonder if these GIs had ever seen combat! We were approached by a couple of MPs who asked us where the hell we had come from—a third world country? We *were* in a third world country, but in the relative safety and cleanliness of the base.

Those stationed there seemed to be engaged in a different war from mine.

After we loaded our trays with food, we took our places at some of the tables and placed our armaments next to us, on the table tops. I think the GIs, officers, nurses, and whoever else was there were stunned, with their mouths gaped open and their eyes wide.

We were just our normal selves, though, on a typical day of work. Having metal eating utensils was a treat, rather than our normal plastic knives, forks, and spoons. What's more, we were eating freshly-prepared food, not C-rations.

Da Nang Air Base, South Vietnam

Da Nang Air Base in South Vietnam was used by both the South Vietnamese and U.S. Forces during the Vietnam War. At the time, it was one of the busiest airports in the world and handled over 2,500 flights per day.

Gunship

Gunship Image by artist John O. Wehrle, CAT I, 1996

Image is in the public domain, courtesy of the National Museum of the U.S. Army, U.S. Combat Art Program

As 1970 gave way to 1971, holiday season was approaching and I chose not to go for R and R (Rest and Relaxation)—not to get away to the safety of Bangkok or Switzerland, to escape from hell. Instead, I went on a mission to find my own peace. I had permission to take the six-hundred-mile journey to spend Christmas Eve with Esmer's brother, Jimmy, who was in the Marine Corps in Vietnam. Esmer was the love of my life, and being close to her brother would make me feel close to her.

Though I was trying to stay alive for my family, my love for that beautiful girl kept me going each day. She was the trophy who made me the envy of everyone back home. So, I set out on this mission to be with Jimmy, her flesh and blood. I obtained my commander's okay to set off for Jimmy's duty station in 'Nam to spend the holiday with him.

Traveling on my own from one end of that war-torn country to the other was both scary and dangerous, but being a seasoned combat veteran bolstered my courage. It was my strength against all odds for accomplishing my mission of seeing Jimmy. I caught helicopter rides, walked alone for hours, sat in the back of half-track vehicles when I could hitch a ride, moved on foot through villages in plain sight of natives, whether friend or foe, and sometimes I was crazy with fear. My locked and loaded M-16 rifle, along with my holstered 45 at my hip and a fully loaded cartridge belt around my waist, served as my security blanket. I often wondered if baffled natives asked themselves, "Who is this lone soldier with the guts to make his solitary way?"

I wasn't leading a full squad of skirmishers; it was just my shadowy self, praying that no one would turn against me, and that I would find the inner strength to override whatever fear I had. Although I had a slight, five-foot-six, one-hundred-thirty-five-pound self, I felt like an action hero. I had to maintain that mentality because I was an American, relatively tall and proud. Talk about boots on the ground! I wasn't airborne in a chopper with the fear of getting shot down. Instead, I was *walking* into the unknown. In my mind, here on the ground I had Esmer as my guardian angel. I knew I couldn't spend Christmas with her, but I would be with her brother, who was my best friend. Today, I marvel over the things a man will endure for the love of a woman.

Upon arriving at the Marine Corps base camp where Jimmy was assigned, I felt safe. I worked my way around the base with directions from Marines and remember seeing the confusion on their faces seeing someone among them wearing Army Aviator's flight gear.

I imagined what they thought: "Has this guy been shot down and found his way to safety? Is he an escaped POW? Or is he just nuts?" When I entered base headquarters and requested an audience with the commanding officer, staff there flashed the same surprised look at having an army soldier walk in.

I walked into the CO's office, saluted, and introduced myself. He made me feel welcomed, but he seemed a little confused at first. After I explained my journey and my mission, he was dumbfounded, but considered my request to visit Jimmy. The kicker, however, was that Jim's unit was out in the field on a reconnaissance mission and not expected back for days.

Knowing there was a truce in place because it was Christmas Eve, I pleaded with him to consider flying me out to Jim's location in the spirit of the holiday, and let me take my chances. I was relieved when he agreed, but only on condition that I sign a waiver protecting the Marine Corps in the event of an unfortunate incident. I thanked him for his compassion and assured him that I could defend myself if the squad should come under attack. He told me there was a copter due to fly out to deliver supplies and beer to the troops, and I could hitch a ride. As I boarded, I felt safe knowing that I was in my comfort zone and not acting in a door gunner capacity. The flight took only about fifteen minutes, but the energy building in me to land and surprise Jim seemed endless. We landed on a ridge and the marines looked up at me as I stepped out of the chopper in my Army flight suit. They seemed very perplexed.

As I approached the squad camping out in a landing zone, Jim finally recognized me, pointed, and hollered, "I know that guy!" He ran toward me as I ran to him and we embraced with warm bear hugs as if we were long lost brothers, which in a way, we were.

"What are you doing here? How did you get here?" he blurted and repeated the questions.

When the dust settled, we had a wonderful time reminiscing, going all the way back to when we both had to leave home for our separate Vietnam journeys. His eyes swelled with tears when I repeated how much I loved his sister.

We celebrated our reunion by drinking beer and decorating a small tree with both empty beer cans and C-ration containers. That was very different from any Christmas tree we remembered back in the States.

Since we were by a river, we decided to go fishing.

Fishing poles? Lines and hooks? Bait? Forget it.

We were out in the bush where tackle was unavailable, so Mexican ingenuity kicked in. We dropped hand grenades in the water and watched as the fish floated up to the surface.

Oh, the memory of that visit! Yet I don't even remember how I managed to get back to my base, so filled was I with the satisfaction of a "mission accomplished" and having spent the holiday with the brother of the woman I loved. All I could think of was how I couldn't wait to write to Esmer to let her know Jimmy and I spent Christmas together and to remind her of my love.

My world turned to confusion, however. As time went on, Esmer's letters to me hinted at problems between her and my mother. The issues were vague, but I sensed their presence. As I resumed combat missions, any doubt about the solidity of the relationship between Mom and Esmer was the last thing I needed. It added a certain uneasiness that came and went until it was my time to fly the freedom bird—either a Continental Airlines or American Airlines plane—back home at last.

Toward the end of my eleven-month tour of duty in 1971, I was still working in avionics and continued flying combat missions. My MOS with its proper security clearance was valuable, and the Army offered me both a $10,000 re-enlistment bonus, E6 stripes—a promotion—and another year in Vietnam.

It was a tempting offer, but I had to give it a lot of thought. The life expectancy of a door gunner was grimly short. Furthermore, my older brother, Felix, had been asking me for permission to transfer to Vietnam, from Udon, Thailand, where he worked with the Army Security Agency (ASA). Ever since World War II, when practically a whole family of brothers was killed in one incident, the military didn't automatically assign siblings together. If they wanted to be together, they had to mutually agree to it. Yet why take the chance of both of us being killed? What would that do to my mother, waiting for us at home? I refused to put us both at the same level of risk, and did not consent to both of us being together. Between my brother's request and the army's offer, I had a lot to think about at that time.

In the end, I knew my Mom back home was still raising five kids, and living in the projects. She could certainly have used $10,000, but I felt I was tempting fate and declined both the bonus and promotion.

Ernest Garcia sitting on "Appaloosa"

In Vietnam, one of the things the young men in Ernest's company liked to do was drive the jeep. They named it "Appaloosa" for the spirited American horse breed. In this photo, Ernest sits on Appaloosa.

Photo courtesy Ernest Garcia

Cockpit of a Vietnam-era Huey Helicopter

The cockpit of the Vietnam-era Huey helicopter shows the instrumentation. As a avionics specialist, Ernest Garcia was responsible for maintaining the communications equipment on the chopper.

Photo courtesy Ernest Garcia

Scale Model of a POW Cage

Ernest built this scale model of a cage American prisoners-of-war soldiers were often kept in if they were captured by the enemy during the Vietnam War. The model is currently housed in Tijeras, New Mexico, at the Museum of the American Military Family.

Photo courtesy Ernest Garcia

Chapter 4: Coming Home

I was doing some rewiring, working in the tailboom of a Cobra gun ship, as usual, when the company clerk hand-delivered my ETS, or Expiration of Term of Service orders. When I read the orders, I couldn't believe it was almost over! Immediately, it seemed a huge weight lifted from my shoulders, and I was delighted to be released from my Vietnam tour of duty a month earlier than I expected. I was to leave five days later, and from that moment on, I was restricted from flying any more missions. It was the Army's way of protecting short-timers. However, I continued to work on avionics up until the day before I left.

Saying *adios* to everyone at Quảng Trị was difficult. Sure, I was thankful to be going home, but not knowing if my buddies would ever make it home was gut-wrenching, and it was particularly difficult to leave my friend, James. We had been through so much together—to hell and back. The bond we shared just can't be adequately described.

Sometimes I would imagine what it would be like seeing my Mother again, and Esmer. Surely, Mom would cry, but what would Esmer do? Would she be happy to see me and would she be ready to continue where we left off with our lives before I was deployed? I just didn't know.

Before I left for the States, one of the things I wanted to do was to help my hooch maid. After I left, she would remain on base, working for my buddies. I called her baby-san and left her a big wad of money—the U.S. version of currency we used in Vietnam. It was called MPC, or Military Payment Certificates. I gave her a big hug, grabbed my duffle bag, drank in her incredible beauty one more time, and walked out of my quarters for the last time. I was going home.

Thankfully, Felix had already arrived home from Thailand, so I did not need to worry about him. Jimmy, Esmer's brother, had also ended his tour of duty, and gone home. I was the last one of our group to return from Southeast Asia.

Military Payment Certificate (MPC)

MPC is the currency used for payment to certain U.S. military personnel from just after the end of World War II to the end of U.S. engagement in Vietnam. Dates this currency was in use: 1946-1973.

Image is in the public domain

Finally, my departure date arrived. After a year of hell, I was on my way home. I daydreamed of kneeling down and kissing the tarmac on American soil. But I could not help thinking of my fallen comrades who had no option other than to lay face down on the floor of the jungle, kissing enemy dirt. My return home was both a moment of wonder and the beginning of many years of torment over the fickleness of destiny. Why had I survived? Why had others died?

Waiting for my flight, I sat on the hangar floor and leaned against the wall, seeking a way to pray. I could not shake the thought of having actually survived my tour of duty, and was getting ready to board a flight home. I was alive, able to walk tall, and my thoughts were of home and Esmer, and our life together as husband and wife.

Another solder spotted me sitting there on the floor as I soaked in the infamous Vietnamese heat for a few last moments.

"Do you want company?" he asked.

"Sure," I replied.

We reminisced about our year at war, and felt a little guilty sitting there, alive, with our buddies either dead or left behind to carry on the battle. Would those still fighting be as lucky as we were, when they finally are advised of their ETS? We would never know.

Finally, we boarded our Continental Airlines "freedom bird" for the long journey home. When the tires of the airplane lifted from the runway in 'Nam, everyone was still apprehensive. Would the North Vietnamese shoot us down? Once the captain announced we had gained a safe altitude, the dozens of us going home broke out in laughter, hugs, and high-fives. We faced hours of flight and many fueling stops before landing in the U.S.

When we finally landed in Seattle, the happy outcry sounded as if we were in a Texas stadium and the Cowboys scored a touchdown. But we were just a planeload of veterans going wild with joy. When we deplaned, many of us knelt down and kissed the tarmac. U.S. soil. I was one of them.

45

The rest of my journey took me to McAllen. I had not told anyone at home I was returning, so it would be a surprise. As I sat on the commercial flight crossing the U.S., I might as well have been a fly on the wall. Not one civilian passenger acknowledged me in any way, or welcomed me home, or thanked me for my service. I was invisible.

I was no longer wearing combat fatigues, but was decked out in my heavily starched Khaki uniform. I stood tall. I stood proud.

* * *

When I landed in McAllen and stepped outside of the terminal, it finally hit me that I was home. I took a deep breath, watched some reunions, and drank in the hustle and bustle of people coming and going. Compared to where I had just come from, it was like stepping out of the Twilight Zone and into a safe haven. I hailed a cab and headed to the Rexall drug store, where Mom worked. On the ride to the store, I was amazed at the growth of McAllen.

The taxi driver asked me where I had just come from, and when I told him I had just returned from Vietnam, there was no acknowledgement from him or any further talk between us.

There were absolutely no signs of our country being at war. War? What war? It seemed the war was very far away to people.

When I arrived at Rexall, everyone was going about their normal business until a co-worker nudged Mom, who was busy restocking cosmetics. I will never forget the look on her face when she gazed at me and it registered that I was her son, standing before her. She ran from the counter to greet me.

"Ernie!" she cried. "Why didn't you tell me you were coming home?"

"I wanted to surprise you!"

Mom dragged me around to all her co-workers, proud to see me in my uniform, and ecstatic I was home at last. All the while she could not stop crying and her manager gave her the rest of the day off, with this order: "Go home with your son!"

Naturally, I was anxious to get to Esmer's house to surprise her, too. To hold her. Mom and I agreed to meet at home in a few hours, and she did leave work early. I called a cab to take me from the Rexall drug store to Esmer's place. My hands were sweaty, anticipating seeing her, Jim, and their loving family.

When the taxi pulled up in front of Esmer's house, she must have been looking out the window, because she ran out of the house, put her arms around me, and hugged and kissed me. She shed happy tears. Holding Esmer in my arms was exhilarating. She was my beautiful woman...my life.

Back at home that night, Mom cooked me the most delicious ribeye steak I had ever eaten. What a difference from C Rations! I enjoyed the time with my little brothers and marveled at how they had grown, although I was a little sad I had missed some of their childhood years.

That day provided a joyous reunion with my Mom and siblings, and Esmer and her family. It was great to see Jimmy again. We talked about our Christmas reunion in 'Nam, and old times together, before either of us was deployed. He had already restarted his country music band and was the lead guitar player. Jimmy had never lost his magic with that instrument and his spider-like magical fingers could weave music together like no one else.

I was on thirty days leave before I had to report to Fort Sill, Oklahoma, to formally terminate my commitment to the Army. I intended to spend every minute of those thirty days with Esmer, friends, and family.

I had an army cot in Jimmy's room and would spend weekend nights at his house, especially on long weekends when I had enough time to travel back and forth between Fort Sill and McAllen. Esmer's room was just a few steps down the hall, but I always refrained from going there out of respect for her and her family.

47

I realized I loved her parents and would never dishonor them by knocking on Esmer's bedroom door.

During those months when I was stationed at Fort Sill and took every chance I could to travel to visit Esmer in McAllen, little by little, I noticed the twinkle in her long-lashed eyes was disappearing. It slowly became clear to me she would never look at me with sparkling eyes again—eyes that could light up a room, especially when we all got together with her family for a musical session, where she would sing directly to me.

One Saturday evening I asked her to accompany me to a country western dance where Jimmy and his band were playing, but she declined with no explanation...just a blank stare. I went to the dance alone, my mind torn all night until Jimmy and I returned home at 2 a.m. After a beer or two, we retired for the night. I lay on the cot for about an hour, thinking and tearing my heart out, wondering what had happened. What had I done? What was wrong with her? What was wrong with me?

Finally, I got up, turned on the light, and woke up Jimmy.

"What the hell are you doing?" he asked.

I was already packing my stuff. "Jim," I said, "talk to your sister. Tell her I can't go on this way. Let me make my point clear. Esmer is just a few feet away, but I can't bring myself to go in there. I'm confused and hurt, not knowing what's going on with her. So I'm out of here."

Jim tried his best to talk me out of leaving, but it didn't work.

I went on, blurting out words about serving my country just as he had, and having no idea what I did to deserve losing her. I mentioned she was the only thing that kept me going in Vietnam, and the reason I survived the horror was because of my love for her, and my desire to come home to her.

Finally, I said, "In my heart I cannot live in the same town and not have her. Wherever I wind up, I will call you and give you my phone number. If she wants to reach out and talk with me, tell her I'm waiting."

My mind was made up.

Throwing all of my belongings in my car, I said goodbye to Jimmy, gave him a special message to relay to Esmer, then got in my car and hit the road. It was 3 a.m.

I thought of a line from F. Scott Fitzgerald's *The Crack-up*:

> "In a real dark night of the soul it is always three o'clock in the morning."

It described perfectly how I felt.

As I pushed the Coronet's 383 Magnum V8 north across the lonely desert road, Highway 281, a Mickey Newberry song played on the radio that also reflected my mood perfectly. I felt I was wound so tightly, that I couldn't unwind, and that my mind might break.

That tune played at just the right moment and filled a deep, dark hole in my mind as I drove that desolate highway. I was writing a movie in my mind, starring Esmer and me. In the movie where she would realize how wrong she had been and she would beg me to come back to her. Somehow, peace of mind and safety would ensue when we would be together again.

There is a great tradition in Hispanic literature called "magical realism" where something unreal will invade reality and coexist along with the real world. That romantic movie playing in my head was definitely from the magical realism school of thought.

As I rolled North, listening to the radio, the window down, and the wind blowing through the Coronet, the darkness reminded me of night missions in Vietnam, of not knowing what the darkness had in store for me. Was night my friend or my enemy? Was the decision I had just made to leave my life behind in McAllen a friend or a foe? And really, how much could I leave behind?

How much could any combat veteran really leave behind?

I settled into a cockroach-infested motel in east Dallas, dazed that such a sweet homecoming could have turned so sour.

Even worse, when I got to Dallas the next morning and knocked on the front door of my brother Felix's apartment, it was clear he could not accommodate me in his small rented place. Although he tried to help, it just wasn't feasible.

I knew I had to find my own way and not encroach on his space. Being a true brother, he did reach out to help me and I persuaded him I would be fine and would be in touch.

However, I wasn't fine at all, and lived in my car for a few days. It was another low point in my life.

I had become a homeless veteran.

But, eventually I did find my own place, and realized that since I had gotten myself into such a sorry situation, I also had to man-up and chart a way out of it.

Besides, I figured that if I could find my own way across Vietnam to visit Jimmy the Christmas I was in-country, I could trust myself to overcome this downtown, too.

* * *

I could not get Esmer off my mind. What was I to do without the love of my life? There was her beauty. There were those weekends we took long drives, her sitting next to me while we held hands. On Sunday afternoon's we'd hand wash my beautiful gold '68 Dodge Coronet, laughing, listening to country music. We'd top off the afternoon by driving to the local botanical gardens for long walks where I enjoyed both her beauty and the loveliness of the flowers.

There was also, Jimmy, my friend. Would we remain friends now that my time with Esmer had come to an end? Would I lose my friendship with him, also?

I stood there at the intersection of Walk or Don't Walk. I decided to take a step forward, and make a new beginning.

With nothing but plenty of time to think, I came to terms with reality. I had to find my way without Esmer. I had to find a job and started looking through the want ads.

Thanks to my veteran status, I secured a job on the graveyard shift as a security officer at the First National Bank on Elm Street in Downtown Dallas.

A Dodge Coronet's 383 Magnum V8

This is a photo of a Dodge Coronet 383 Magnum V8, like the one I owned when I left McAllen. Mine was painted a gold color.

Photo by Ernest Garcia

Chapter 5: The Bank, Dilyla, and the Oilfields

After Vietnam, after Esmer, I headed for Dallas and secured my first post-war job there, at First National Bank of Dallas. I was a security officer and worked the graveyard shift for three years, then transferred to day shift, and then was promoted to shift supervisor in charge of the main banking lobby. From 1972 until 1979, I had the privilege of working for Mr. Paul Bentley while at the bank. Paul was one of the arresting detectives of Lee Harvey Oswald, when he worked for the Dallas Police Department. In a stroke of good fortune, Paul took me under his wing, taught me about banking security, and exposed me to behind-the-scene activities at the bank.

At that time, it was somewhat common in Dallas for CEOs and other executives to become kidnap victims. Paul was frequently invited as a speaker on issues regarding security training and protection of executives. He was not only a former detective, and a famous one at that, but also a security consultant. I remember one of the suggestions he offered regarding security for executives: avoid taking the same driving route from home to the office and back again on a routine basis. Vary it, and avoid becoming a predictable creature of habit, to deter kidnappers.

Whenever a executive kidnapping did occur, the FBI would often turn to Paul and the bank for help. He always made it a point to involve me and I witnessed bank officials and FBI personnel marking and counting millions of dollars of ransom money.

He always encouraged me to build and maintain contacts which could help me in my career and throughout life. Good advice. He got me involved as a member of the nationwide brotherhood, the National Society for Industrial Security. We would attend monthly conferences at major hotels where I met

Secret Service and FBI agents, polygraph examiners—Paul was a renowned polygraph examiner—and a wide spectrum of the law enforcement community, including many other local Security Administrators. These contacts could help me make my mark in the industry, and could lead to being offered a high level security position at another bank or in another industry.

One day, while I was working in the main banking lobby, he asked me to take a walk with him. We left the building, and before I realized it, we were walking into the Federal Reserve Bank. With his reputation, he seemed to have *carte blanche* and could move in the highest security areas of the Federal Reserve Bank. He gave me a tour of the place, where I saw money being printed as well as shredded. He managed to find and give me a glass vile of shredded bills as a keepsake. His primary reason for the visit to that bank was to purchase a $500 bill in mint condition as a gift for his wife on their anniversary.

One of the benefits of working at the bank was the opportunity to meet many players of the Dallas Cowboys football team. I met Bob Hayes, Calvin Hill, Walt Garrison, Jethro Pugh, Roger Stauback, Harvey Martin, Tom Landry, Drew Pearson, Preston Pierce, Robert Newhouse, Tony Hill, Steelers Head Coach George Allen, Ed Too Tall Jones, Tony Dorsett—a Heisman Trophy winner. His Heisman Trophy display was carefully guarded in our main banking lobby.

Harvey Martin was one of my favorites because every time he was in the bank lobby, he always stopped to visit with me. I thought his thighs were larger than my waist, and his nickname, "The Gentle Giant," suited him well.

On the weekends, I would often go to Wichita Falls to some dance halls or watering holes; it was a practice I had started with some friends when I was in the last few months of military service in Lawton, Oklahoma. We always had a fun time on our weekends in Texas and we met a lot of nice young women. After my breakup with Esmer, I developed a relationship with Dilyla, and she and I married in 1972. I am not certain if I married her because I was on the rebound from Esmer, but I adored Dilyla, and our daughter was born in 1975. It seemed like my life was full and I was settling down, but money was always tight.

I was a husband and father with a deep sense of responsibility to my new family. It was time for me to think of our future.

Despite Paul's taking me under his wing and exposing me to security aspects of the banking industry I might not have known without him, I needed to earn a higher wage and resigned from my job at the bank for, eventually, a much more lucrative one in the oil fields. Paul was disappointed, but it was a decision I had to make.

Paul Bentley was a giant of man. I will always remember him as my mentor, my boss, and my friend. Although he died in 2008, I treasure the relationship we had.

* * *

I did not have another job lined up yet when I quit the bank, and my wife was very anxious to move to Wichita Falls, to be near her family. She did not drive and was very dependent on me, so being near her family was more comfortable for her.

I took a job as a parking attendant at Leslie's Parking Garage. The pay was meager. I barely took home $85 a week, hardly enough to pay our bills. We got behind on everything, and I distinctly remember only being able to buy toilet paper one or two rolls at a time, rather than a whole pack.

One of the men who parked his car at the garage was Mr. Bolin, the head of DH Bolin Company, an oil business. Finally, I decided to take a chance. Oil field workers were well paid, and I wanted to be one.

It was a quiet Saturday at the parking garage and Mr. Bolin always worked a while on Saturday. Somehow, I found a bit of courage. On my lunch break, I crossed the street and took the elevator to his office. My heart pounded in my chest as I stood outside his office door. I knocked and walked in.

"Ernest, is everything OK?" he asked as he saw me.

"Yes, sir, it is. May I talk with you if you have a minute?"

"Sure, have a seat," he responded.

I took a deep breath. I *had* to ask him for a job. It was impossible trying to live on my inadequate salary and tips.

"Mr. Bolin, thank you. You know where I work—Leslie's Garage?"

He nodded.

"As you might imagine, it is not a high paying job, sir. The fact of the matter is, my family is nearly starving. I take home less than $90 a week. I've come to you in desperation."

Mr. Bolin remained quiet, and let me speak.

"Mr. Bolin, I have come to you to let you know I want to work for you, and won't take 'No' for an answer, sir. All I ask is that you give me a chance."

"Ernest," he replied, "do you have any idea what it takes to work in the oilfields?"

"No, not really," I responded, "but all I ask is to give me a chance." I continued, "Sir, give me two weeks. If you are not satisfied with my work, you don't have to pay me. Give me a chance. I promise you I can handle anything you throw at me. That's how hungry we are. I can't take 'No' for an answer. I just can't."

Mr. Bolin rested back in his chair, looked me directly in the eye, and picked up the phone.

He dialed a number, and I heard, "Arky, I am sending you Ernest from Leslie's Garage. He is to report for work in the pipe yard on Monday morning."

Arky must have been saying something to Mr. Bolin, because all I heard was, "Yes, Ernest, that's right...the fellow from the parking lot. Put him to work and see how he does. Show him the ropes and give him a chance." I later learned Arky was the foreman of the pipe yard.

A big lump swelled in my throat. A sense of relief, of hope, enveloped me and I was glad I had taken the chance to approach Mr. Bolin. I wondered why it took me so long to talk him.

I stood up and faced Mr. Bolin. "Thank you, sir. Thank you for this opportunity. I won't let you down."

We shook hands warmly. I don't know how he felt, but I was on Cloud 9, but scared.

Would I really be able to stand up to my promise of not letting him down? Would I be able to do the work well?

I was on a roller coaster of emotions.

When I informed my manager at the parking garage that I was quitting—and why—he was very happy for me, and acknowledged there was really no future at Leslie's.

As I drove home, I realized I had to tell Dilyla that I had quit my job for something unknown. Mostly, I wanted her to trust me that I did what I thought was the right thing for us.

I walked into the bedroom, where she was cuddling our daughter, and told her I was no longer employed at the garage. The look on her face was full of fear. I told her what I had done, and she was still concerned, especially with my offering to work for free for two weeks, and if it didn't work out, not having another job.

* * *

I worked for two weeks under the supervision of Arky, fully expecting to be unpaid, as I had offered Mr. Bolin. But at the end of those two weeks, Arky handed me an envelope with a check inside. That afternoon, I cashed the check and Dilyla cried with relief when I handed her $1,500.

"I just needed you and Mr. Bolin to believe in me," I said.

With my new high-paying job, we were able to get caught up on all our bills.

Portable Oil Drilling Unit, or Spudder

An example of a movable spudder, or oil drilling unit similar in concept to those Ernest Garcia worked on in the oilfields.

Richard Thornton/ Shutterstock.com

I worked for five years in the oil fields of DH Bolin Company, from 1979-1982, and they were very eventful five years.

I started in the pipe yard, and Arky, the yard foreman, trusted me. He allowed me to drive the company truck and sometimes sent me to a town called Cement, Oklahoma. It was a small town, and it was eye-opening to me to see pumping units in front yards, backyards, and almost in the middle of the street. Everywhere you turned there were these shallow well units on old existing wells that had been drilled in past years. DH Bolin owned and operated about 300 of these wells. I would drive there to deliver parts to our oil field crews.

There were various times I was sent to Cement to work alongside with the crews when they were short-handed. I experienced working on those work-over rigs—a dirty job. When pipe is pulled out of the ground, with it comes chemical additives that were placed in the bore hole. It would spray all over us. Most of us shopped at places such as Goodwill to purchase shirts and pants for as little as twenty-five or fifty cents. We would arrive fresh to those well sites, strip down, and then change into those cheap clothes to work on the spudders— portable cable drilling rigs. By noon we would strip again, because our clothes were filthy. Before we left the site, we would dump all the dirty clothing in a pile and burn it to ashes. Then, we would go back to work and expect to get filthy two or three more times, each time burning the hopelessly dirtied clothing. At day's end, we would hose each other down to get the muck off our bodies.

I also worked as a truck swamper, hauling drill pipe and equipment, and moving oil storage tanks. I tore down the entire doubles and triples to move the rig to the new location. My driver, Jack Sears, and I entertained each other on the long trips by joking and teasing each other. He nicknamed me Pasquale, probably because we drove a Peterbuilt rig and the name fit. The biggest challenge was to truck an entire derrick as one unit. This method required the lead truck to transport the top part of the derrick mounted on it in unison with another truck behind it that carried the end of the derrick. The second truck had to drive backwards all the way! Whether it was snowing, pouring rain, or spawning tornadoes, the show had to go on. Eventually, I got to work on the big rigs as a roughneck, taking on the role of chain hand. I managed the heavy chain that helped all the connections in the rig work. I was on the night shift, which started at 7:00 p.m. and ended at 7:00 a.m. Oh, I loved being a roughneck. Once the work got into my blood, I was proud and hooked on it.

Roughnecks at Work

"Roughneck" is the term used for someone who performs hard physical labor, usually on an oil rig in various capacities, including drillers, chainhands, boilermen, derrickhands, motormen, and more.

Image is in the public domain

On April 10, 1979, I was working with my crew when DH Bolin's Operations at Wichita Falls kept informed us via radio of a weather situation that was brewing. We were drilling in Bowie, Texas, not quite fifty miles out of Wichita Falls, and the tornado watches quickly turned into tornado warnings. The crew's driller radioed back and asked for permission to cease drilling and allow us all to head home. Permission was granted. We drove as fast as we could through high winds, hail, and black rolling low clouds. The sky was ominous, and although it was officially daytime, it looked like nightfall. I was about a half mile from my mother-in law's house when the tornado sirens started screaming. I gathered all members of my family in my van, and we raced to Sid Peterson Hospital, where there was an underground shelter.

Halfway there, large, heavy, vertical-falling hail slammed on my van, and when we arrived at the hospital, we were among many people seeking shelter. There were abandoned vehicles everywhere—on the sidewalks, in the street, anywhere. It was chaos. By that time, three tornados had merged into one giant monster.

All hell had broken loose, and we headed to the basement. Terrified women and children were crying.

Fortunately, I had a small transistor radio and I shared weather updates with everyone. I could hear the reports of the tornado's path through the city. Everyone was worried about their homes and neighbors, and not knowing made us extremely anxious.

Victims began to arrive, and the hospital staff asked for help unloading the injured from cars, ambulances, and even the beds of pickup trucks. Immediately, all of us men jumped up to help the doctors and nurses. I remember it as if it just happened yesterday. I especially recall one large man in the back of a pickup. He had 2 x 4 length of wood lodged in his thigh. A few days later I returned to the hospital to check up on him as he was recovering, and he was very thankful.

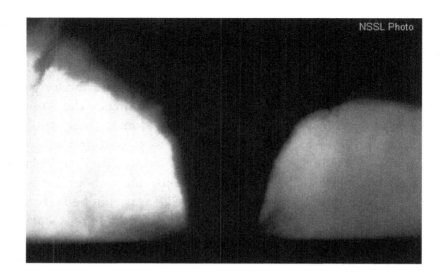

April 10, 1979 Tornado

The EVF 4 tornado that hit Wichita Falls on April 10, 1979, caused widespread damage. All Ernest Garcia, his wife, and child had left was the clothing on their backs and their little dog.

Photo courtesy of National Severe Storms Laboratory

Aftermath of Wichita Falls Tornado on 4/10/1979

Ernest and his family survived the tornado that left near complete destruction in its path, and the loss of forty-two people in Wichita Falls, Texas. It became known as "Terrible Tuesday" in the annals of weather disasters.

Photo courtesy of National Oceanic and Atmospheric Administration

The morning after the tornado, we could return to our neighborhoods to check on our homes and belongings. Driving through a battlefield of heavy debris, downed telephone poles, uprooted trees, and cars destroyed to rubble, we finally made it home to our duplex. The roof was gone, and oddly, our bedroom closet was still intact, with clothes still on the hangers. Dilyla and I had just purchased new furniture for the living room, and it, along with all our other furniture, was gone. The smell of gas from broken natural gas lines permeated the air, and we were very concerned that live electrical wires might be in the mess that used to be our home. We frantically searched for our little dog, and as I combed through the rubble, I opened the doors to the storage area under the kitchen sink and found our Maltese puppy shaking like a leaf. I guess he instinctively sought shelter, since we were unable to catch him when we left before the tornado hit. We had almost nothing material left but we did have our dog.

All my original military medals from Vietnam were gone, but the questions on everyone's mind were: "What do we do now?" and "Where are we going to live?"

Word was out that any veteran affected by the disaster should report to a specific location, a makeshift shelter sponsored by the DAV (Disabled American Veterans). I identified myself and was escorted to a table. They verified my veteran status and handed me a check for $500. I was speechless and their generosity brought me to tears. I owe a lot to the DAV organization for giving me hope, and have been a life member since 1983.

After the tornado, my wife, daughter, and I stayed with my mother-in-law for a while. As part of its disaster relief programs, FEMA (Federal Emergency Management Agency) housed us in a motel, but then set up temporary housing in Kiwanis Park in large trailer-type homes. We were there for one year, rent-free, and with free utilities. We stayed in Wichita Falls and moved into a nice apartment after our time in the trailer.

Today, when I look back on that awful tornado, I realize that seeing my little dog shaking under the kitchen sink triggered what later became known as PTSD (Post Traumatic Stress Disorder). The poor pup was trembling violently, just as my legs shook uncontrollably when I was shooting an M-60 out of a helicopter in Vietnam.

Yet I was grateful I was in the United States, where help was available. The community came together to support the victims of the tornado.

Trailer Home Provided by FEMA

FEMA provided the family a three-bedroom trailer which they lived in for a year after the tornado struck Wichita Falls.

Photo courtesy Ernest Garcia

We recovered from the tornado, and in 1983, I went to work for another oil company, Linn-Mour Drilling, also as a roughneck.

Being a roughneck is not only dirty, but also physically grueling. In winter, temperatures often dropped to single digits. Rain, snow, ice, and wind tortured us. The wind was especially unbearable, and under our coveralls we wore long johns, two or three shirts, and two pairs of pants, all to stave off the wind chill.

Yet working on those monster rigs was breathtaking. The activity of drilling for oil was exciting, and when you struck oil, it was rewarding to see the results of your demanding work. One of our jobs was to collect drilling samples and examine them under a black light. We would see that "Texas gold" had come to light. When we found oil in the samples, we would radio for a geologist to come to our location. When the geologist confirmed that we had, indeed, found oil, we could quickly get all the land owners and investors to pay us a visit and celebrate with lots of liquor and champagne. We roughnecks had, after all, just made them richer.

* * *

I worked long hours on night shift and spent a lot of time on the road. On the morning of December 15th, 1983, I arrived at my mother-in-law's house, where my wife was spending the night. My mother-in-law informed me Dilyla seemed to be ill. I found my wife incoherent and rushed her to the hospital, where nurses and doctors immediately took her into the emergency room. After a couple of hours of tests, the doctor came out to talk to me and told me the staff was baffled trying to determine what was going on with my wife. Only an hour after that talk, she was in a coma and it appeared that her organs were shutting down. As the hours passed, all her family arrived from out of town and that evening, the doctors met us and informed us that she was legally brain dead. Only life support was sustaining her heart and breathing.

The doctors counseled me: as her husband, I needed to decide whether to keep her on life support or not. I gathered the family for help in making such a difficult and critical decision. Dilyla and I had discussed that if anything happened to either one of us, we wished not to be placed on long-term life support. Yet, that conversation was held in the abstract. The choice before me was real, and despite our having talked about life support, it was still the hardest decision of my life. I was also torn because she was leaving me with an eight-year-old daughter to raise by myself.

In the end, I honored Dilyla's wishes, and gave permission to disconnect all the life support equipment. She died peacefully, with her family around her.

Linn-Mour Drilling Company offered and paid for her funeral. They were wonderful and so supportive, a company with heart.

There it was, less than two weeks before Christmas, and I was burying my thirty-year-old wife in the snow.

* * *

After Dilyla's burial I would sometimes jump the cemetery fence in the middle of the night, and cry at her grave until I was spent and fell asleep.

Out in the oilfield, I would occasionally tell the driller I could not handle the night shift, leave the rig in the middle of the night, and hitchhike back to Wichita Falls where we members of the crew kept our vehicles. The dark roadside was frightening and dangerous, punctuated now and then with the mournful sounds of howling coyotes. By sheer force of will, I was determined to get to wife's gravesite, so I pushed forward into the darkness to reach my destination. I'd ride with a truck driver or anyone who had pity for a lonely soul along the roadside.

My driller would try to console me when I broke down at the worksite. In his infinite wisdom he told me, "Ernest, it takes time to get over a tragedy like the loss of a loved one."

My response to him was a simple one. "I know it takes time, but I don't have time. Time has a way of taking its *own* time, and I don't have that luxury." I didn't know how I was going to raise a young daughter by myself. She was only eight years old when Dilyla died. I thought of the growing pains of adolescence, the changes womanhood brings to a girl. I felt ill-equipped to handle them. God help me!

Luckily, I had Dilyla's family as a support system. My niece, my wife's cousin, took us in for a year to help me raise my daughter while I was working graveyard shift at the oil fields. I am forever grateful to Johnny and Lila for all they did and sacrificed for us. I can never forget their kindness and I am certain God blesses them.

* * *

I decided to leave Wichita Falls and return to McAllen. It was just too painful for me to stay where Dilyla had died. I knew I was facing an unknown future with my daughter and giving up the option to visit my wife's grave whenever I wanted.

Would Dilyla have approved?

I don't know, but just as I had to leave the same town where I lost Esmer, I could no longer stay in the town where I had lost Dilyla. It took me a year to make the decision, and I can remember my driller's words to me at my weakest moments, "Ernest, it's going to take time."

Chapter 6: Back to McAllen

When I returned to McAllen, I worked as a meat cutter for a while, when I met my second wife. We married about a year and a half later. During our years together, my daughter bonded to her, and I signed on with Jen Craft Corporation at a *maquiladora* in Reynosa, Mexico across the border. The maquiladora manufactured mini blinds with material imported from another country, often duty- and tariff-free. I commuted between the US and Reynosa.

I was hired as a plant superintendent for the night shift. Jen Craft was a major supplier of mini blinds, and I oversaw the operations and production of approximately 300 employees. I had to quickly learn both the mini blind manufacturing process and the culture of Mexican workers. It was a challenge.

The workers were from all walks of life, poor, and usually uneducated. Determining who needed hugging, who needed a spanking, and who did something that made me have to put out a fire—a crisis—kept me on my toes. But probably the most serious trials came from the union. The workers were under union control, but their wages were the lowest I had ever seen. If memory serves me right, the average pay was $7.00 per day.

At the factory, we produced quality products 99% of the time, but with the workers under union control, there were some major problems. The union president also worked at our plant and from my perspective, it seemed like there were issues of sabotage against our products. The blinds we manufactured used plastic pellets, and sometimes, we found foreign matter planted in our bails of pellets, and they could cause blue streaks in the blind slats. We were certain the union leadership directed people to contaminate our products, causing us a huge headache with quality control. It was hard to determine exactly who was doing the dirty work for the union, and we never caught the culprits who tampered with the buckets of pellets.

The women workers were afraid of the union president, and therefore loyal to him, even if it was a reluctant loyalty. They had no choice if they wanted to keep their jobs and earn money to support their families, however meager that money was.

Most of the younger pretty girls were at the mercy of the union boss. He had control over them and was not afraid to use his power. We suspected he knew of all the secluded areas of the plant where he would induce them to have sex with him. We did implement some safety measures of control, but I could not be everywhere at the same time in such a huge plant. However, I did notify upper management that he was number one on my radar and eventually I would nail him.

One of the measures I instituted was to control the keys to the bathrooms in each department where I was working. I did this for both the men and the women. When someone needed to use the rest room, the worker came to me and I handed him or her the key; each worker returned the key to me when exiting the rest room.

Knowing what a sly fox the union head was, I kept a close eye on his movements. One night about 5:00 a.m. a young lady came to me for the key. I moved around to where the union boss could not spot me and observed him following that young pretty girl into the bathroom area. I banged on the door, entered the rest room, and caught them in the act. I directed the company security detail to remove each of them to a separate room, and to await the arrival of upper management. Both the female employee and the male union leader were fired, escorted to the plant's gate the same day.

Immediately, word of the firing of the union boss spread like wildfire and there were death threats hurled at me over the coming days. I was warned I would not live long enough to cross the border back into the U.S., where I lived with my wife and daughter. For the remainder of the week I was escorted to and from the border between the U.S. and Mexico. My wife was very concerned for my safety.

After about three years, I resigned from Jen Craft, much to the relief of my wife.

* * *

Like many Vietnam veterans, I turned to the McAllen Veterans Outreach Center to use their database to look for work.

Fortunately, I found a job with the South Texas Can Company as a supervisor in charge of production and quality control. I learned the intricate process of manufacturing cans. However, production ground to a halt during a freeze that diminished the fruit available for canning, and the plant moved to Oklahoma. I chose not to relocate with the plant.

When I worked at South Texas Can Company, management sent me for some Dale Carnegie courses in communications and management. I learned how to build relationships, and how to influence people. I practiced public speaking and was taught how not to be afraid of approaching people.

South Texas Can Company Clothing Patch

Courtesy Ernest Garcia

After leaving the can company, I looked for another job through the Veteran's Outreach Center. I found something quite different for me—selling life insurance door-to-door, a "cold call" if you will, and everything I learned through Dale Carnegie I applied on this job. I became a life insurance agent for Western & Southern Life Insurance Company.

Company headquarters were in Cincinnati and the office I was associated with was in Harlingen, Texas. I turned out to be the gleam in my office manager's eye. Luis Perez taught me how to be tenacious and was a good mentor. I remember one instance in particular, where he was on a business trip to Cincinnati at the home office, but he was embarrassed about going to the meeting there because of declining sales at our office. Before he left for his trip, he said to me, "I need your help; please make me proud while I'm gone."

I took off to Port Isabel to close a business continuity sale with a husband-and-wife business owner team. When I arrived, the wife had finally convinced her husband to sign a contract with me, to insure she could keep the business running in case something happened to him. Across the street from their establishment, another business owner had died unexpectedly, and his business failed. My client—the wife, at least—wanted to make sure that didn't happen to her. As it worked out, I did close the deal with them. I rushed to a pay phone to call it into my office, asking that they forward the news to Mr. Perez at the home office. I knew I had given him something to brag about with the others at that meeting. I do believe this sale was the final piece of a puzzle that resulted in my being named "Rookie of the Year" in 1994. I was honored at a convention in South Padre Island. Each life insurance company, auto insurance company, etc., competed in sales to have one of its agents be honored as Rookie of the Year

Within my first year I was grossing over $4,000 a month, strictly on commission, when many other agents were earning less than $300 per week. Corporate in Cincinnati also praised

Mr. Perez for training the first agent in South Texas to be honored with this prestigious award. I also earned other sales awards, but nothing as exciting as the Rookie award. Afterwards, other insurance companies such as American General, Reliable, and State Farm tried to recruit me, but I would not leave Mr. Perez. He groomed me to be successful and realized I decided to tenaciously pursue success with integrity. He was pushing me to be the first agent in the Texas Rio Grande Valley to earn the Million Dollar Club Award. I was earning $48,000 a year and my wife, $35,000. We had everything, including a beautiful three-bedroom home with a 3/4 acre back yard, beautiful lush green grass, and big oak trees.

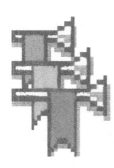

Rookie-of-the-Year Award

Ernest P. Garcia
Western & Southern Life

Ernest Garcia came into the business on January 3, 1994 from a maquiladora supervisory position. 1994 was a very successful year for Mr. Garcia; during this first year in the business he qualified for the National Sales Achievement Award, having generated over $30,000 of first year commission. He will also qualify for the National Quality Award with a 95% persistency.

Ernie has been an exemplary new agent with his cooperation in assisting both the Association and his fellow sales representatives.

Mr. Garcia has also been selected as the Rookie of the Year for the Rio Grande District office of Western & Southern Life. As new to the business as he is, he is presently enrolled in LUTC 1 and the Company's Career Direction Program. He is also a Dale

Rookie of the Year Announcement

This announcement is from the February 1995 issue of *Life Notes*, published by The Valley Association of Life Underwriters.

Document courtesy Ernest Garcia

Life can take unexpected turns, however. My wife and I were going through a tough time, and we initiated divorce proceedings. The turmoil at home affected my performance at work. As a result, I lost my ambition and enthusiasm for my job. With the distractions my personal life forced me to face, Mr. Perez was devastated with my inability to perform in the field. He dreamed he would become the first sales manager in South Texas to develop a Million Dollar Club agent for Western & Southern Life Insurance Company. But, it wasn't to be, both to his disappointment and mine. Nonetheless, I will always appreciate the support and encouragement he offered me when I worked for his office.

Life at the insurance company didn't go the way I had expected. I opted to turn in my resignation for the best of all concerned—my family, and especially my manager, Mr. Perez.

* * *

Job-wise, I moved on. My goal was to dream big and seek state or federal jobs. I applied for the U.S. Postal Service and maxed out the test. Even with veteran's preference I was never selected, and I suspect is was due to the "brother-in-lawing" phenomenon, a practice which I believe awarded jobs to family members of those who already had them. Yet the staff at the Vet Center was composed of Vietnam veterans and they were close friends of mine, offering me both encouragement and help. I would go there regularly and seek work, determined to get a job. One day I walked through the doors and Richard—he was the lead administrative person and knew everything that was going on—eagerly told me there was a position available and he thought I would be just the right person to fill it. He gave me a phone number and told me to call right away.

The phone number was the direct link to the office manager, Teri Lopez Trevino, of Social Security District office. She had called the center seeking Vietnam Veterans to immediately fill eight temporary positions for eight months. The staff had recommended me to the manager and she was waiting for my call for an interview.

At the interview, she hired me on the spot. It was very early in 1989. It was a blessing to finally land a Federal job with the employment security if offered. It was a turning point in my life and bolstered my self esteem and allowed me to provide for my daughter and not depend on my own mother.

The temporary job at Social Security came open because of changes in the Alien Reform Act; that was in 1996. Eight veterans were hired to concentrate solely on examining thousands of paper files. We had to screen each one for special codes that would identify the many Mexican aliens who might be eligible to be grandfathered into the system and be entitled to SSI (Supplemental Income) benefits and Medicaid, as well as regular SSA (Social Security Administration) benefits based on their work history and payments into the system.

My manager was pleased with my work and offered me a new challenge. Due to the heavy work load at the Social Security District office, some priorities had to be placed on the back burner. My new assignment was to go through hundreds of files of potential fraud reports. I had to inspect each one and determine if it warranted my filing an official fraud report to the O.I.G., (Office of the Inspector General). With each report I filed, I had to also email the office manager a copy. After three days, I was on a roll, prompting Mrs. Lopez to come to me. She thanked me for working hard, for taking a deep bite out of the work load.

The only problem that got her attention is that I had filled her in box to the max.

"Be careful what you ask for!" I admonished. I knocked out that work load in a week's time.

At the end of the eight month employment period, Mrs. Lopez pulled all eight of us into her office for a meeting. She informed us that Social Security had lifted a freeze on hiring full-time personnel and that there were openings in Houston and

Gainesville, Texas, Shreveport, Louisiana, and Albuquerque, New Mexico. She was only permitted to hire one of us full-time for her office, and I had hopes of being selected because of my experience and made it clear I was interested in becoming a Federal employee. She encouraged us to submit an application and a resumé to all four locations. Based on the orders Mrs. Lopez received, hiring priority had to go to a disabled veteran. One veteran in our group had polio and got the placement.

I wanted to stay at the McAllen, Texas office for the sake of my marriage of thirteen years. Although my wife and I were in the process of divorcing, we also made some attempts at reconciliation. Ultimately, we did not get back together again, and divorced.

It turned out to be good timing to make a change, and I elected to go to the Houston Teleservice Center. My older brother and one of my sisters lived there, and I needed to be with family for support. Mrs. Lopez told me I qualified for all four cities to which I applied and questioned me as to why I chose Houston. We discussed my decision and she told me that although Houston was ready to hire me, I might wish to consider another venue because of the need for certified bilingual employees and better chances for promotion.

The Houston office was already well-staffed with bilingual Hispanics and that fact prompted me to consider Albuquerque, New Mexico instead. Since I was mobile, I decided to take the job but asked Mrs. Lopez, "Where in the hell is Albuquerque?" I vaguely remembered reading about Albuquerque in junior high school, but had no idea how to get there. She told me not to worry; she was confident that I would do well in the largest city in New Mexico. That was on a Tuesday. She informed me I would be off Friday, giving me three days to pack up and get to Albuquerque, find an apartment, and report to the Social Security Teleservice Center the following Monday at 8:00 a.m.

And so, I began a new chapter of my life.

Chapter 7: Albuquerque

Before I left Texas for New Mexico in September of 1989, all my friends were teasing me that the only women I would find in New Mexico would be Native Americans. They would be ugly, I was told. The drive was long—somewhere between eleven and thirteen hours. When I crossed the Texas border into New Mexico, I stopped to stretch my legs and buy gasoline. The clerk behind the counter was very attractive; she was beautiful. I paid for my purchase, and half way back to my truck, I pivoted sharply and walked back to talk to her.

"Are you a Native American?" I asked her.

"Yes, I am," she said.

I laughed and saw a questioning look on her face, her eyebrows raised.

"My co-workers back in Texas told me all Native women are ugly, but you just proved them a hundred percent wrong. You are really beautiful."

She blushed at my comment and thanked me, and I went on my way. I should have ignored the comments of my buddies back in Texas!

What I noticed most about New Mexico was the variety of the land. It wasn't all flat. There were hills and mesas, arroyos and towering mountains, quaint towns and cities. It was quite different from the flat lands in the part of the Texas where I had lived.

I arrived in Albuquerque on a Friday night and pulled off I-25 at the first motel I saw—The Crossroads Motel. All these years later, it is still in business. After a good night's sleep, I awakened with a major task to accomplish: finding a place to live. I found an apartment right away through an agency. By now I was really hungry for a good meal. I stopped at a restaurant and ordered something called *carne adovada*, a marinated pork dish that is very popular in New Mexico. What I later learned was considered "normal" for my newly-adopted state, the meat was smothered in a red sauce I thought looked like dog puke. I was told it was red chile sauce. I took one bite of the meal, and spit it out, paid my bill, and left the restaurant. I think I found a burger place and ate something. The following day I went to Old Town, the historic center of Albuquerque, where a tree-covered center square was lined with old buildings, including San Felipe Church. Other adobe structures housed charming shops. My friends back in McAllen had told me to go there, and they were right about its being attractive, even then were wrong about the Native women. I stopped at a restaurant and figured I would try carne adovada without the red stuff on top. This time, it was smothered in green chile sauce. Again, I did not eat it and found a place to buy a burger. To this day, I do not like food smothered in chile sauce of any color or heat intensity!

Moving to Albuquerque coincided with a love interest I had while still in McAllen. A client of mine when I was a life insurance agent became my third wife. I travelled to McAllen to marry her and she relocated to Albuquerque along with her two sons from a previous marriage. During our years together, the eldest son moved back to Texas to be with his father, but the boys' dad committed suicide. I had the task—a painful and difficult one—of telling the younger son, who was at school, what had happened. All of us went to the funeral, and I moved the oldest son back to New Mexico. Our marriage lasted five years before we divorced; my ex-wife and her sons moved back to McAllen.

* * *

My work at the Social Security Teleservice Center in Albuquerque began with sixteen weeks of intensive training. I learned how to answer the questions of people who called, and since I am bilingual, I could help both English-speaking and

Spanish-speaking callers. Inquires from clients ranged the full spectrum of anything someone might want to ask Social Security. We had books and books of reference materials to refer to as we answered questions.

Not only did I have my full-time job at Social Security Administration, but I also signed on as a part time meat cutter with both Sam's Club and Smith's grocery stores when I first arrived in Albuquerque. As it turned out, I worked so many hours at Sam's Club that it was really another full-time job.

One of the most memorable things I did at Sam's Club was to help the teenage son of a fellow employee. The lad was selected to go to Australia to compete against Australian High School football players. However, he would need to raise $5,000 for the trip and that was a sum his mother could not handle, and there were no family members able to come up with the money. I decided to help and spearheaded the effort to raise funds for the boy's trip to Australia. A local printer agreed to print the tickets for the fundraiser, after I told them the story. Sam's management and other companies donated raffle items.

We met the $5,000 goal and off went our football player to the Land Down Under. It was very gratifying for me, and to thank me, the young fellow's mother invited me to the family home in Las Vegas, New Mexico. At one point during my visit, we decided to take a walk on her father's acreage. As we explored the land, I ran across a goat skull in a field. It intrigued me, and I asked if I could keep it. They agreed. It had two very nice antlers, but I had no idea what I was going to do with it. I just knew I wanted it.

As it turned out, I placed it on my truck's dashboard. I got attached to this silly old skull and often talked to it, telling it my problems and feelings whether I was driving to work or to someplace in the beautiful New Mexico mountains. But the skull needed a name. I remembered seeing the movie *Castaway* with Tom Hanks, who was alone on a deserted island for several years. He had a volleyball from the Federal Express cargo plane he was on when the airplane crashed in the ocean. He and some of the cargo, including the ball, wound up on the shore of the island. He talked to the ball all the time, and called it "Wilson" while on the island. I named my goat skull "Wilson" just as Tom Hanks named his volleyball. I talked to Wilson when I was still adjusting to my life in a new state, pondering whether to divorce my third wife. People used to ask me why I mounted the skull on the dashboard. I would tell them it was a true friend, always listened, and never talked back. Yet some of my co-workers told me it looked satanic! Eventually, I no longer needed the skull. I removed it from the dashboard, but keep it in my office.

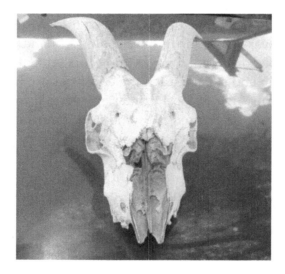

Wilson

Ernest named this goat skull he found on a walk "Wilson" to use as a companion to talk to, similar to the volleyball Tom Hanks used in the film, *Castaway*.

Photo by Patricia Walkow

I worked at the Social Security Administration Service Center in Albuquerque for almost eighteen years, and during that time our reference materials and call processes were converted from paper to computers. I gained much knowledge and almost fulfilled my goal of retiring after twenty-five years. But fate intervened.

* * *

February 1st, 2008 was a Saturday morning. I awakened with what felt like a charley horse—spasms and cramps—in my lower left leg. It was a gradual pain that turned to a growing numbness that extended to my foot. I tried to shake it off; I tried walking; I tried massaging my leg. Nothing helped. Concerned, I pulled out a VA (Veterans Administration) card with a list of phone numbers. I mentioned to my wife that something was wrong, and then called the emergency medical number on the card. I was connected to a help line in Dallas (I was in Albuquerque), and the nurse at the other end of the line listened very intently as I described my symptoms. She told me I was in a very urgent situation and should get to the VA Hospital immediately. I distinctly remember her telling me that if I had not yet shaved or showered, that I shouldn't, and go right away or call an ambulance. She told me she would be calling the hospital and they would expect me to be there shortly. I was not to drive, but to call for assistance or have someone drive me.

Being the stubborn man that I am, I took a shower anyway and even drove as far as the freeway exit ramp, but then had my stepson take over.

At the hospital, I was seen right away and diagnosed with an aneurysm—a bulge filled with blood inside the wall of a blood vessel—behind the knee cap. It was slightly larger than the size of a quarter. The doctor told me I presented as a textbook case and asked me to sign a consent form allowing him to use my case as training for his residents, and to present it at a medical conference in Arizona, along with photos of the surgery. I readily consented, since it meant it could help other people. After I gave my consent to surgery, the doctor told me what the worst-case scenarios would be: if the blood clot had traveled to my heart, I could have died; it might have been necessary to amputate the leg from the knee down. As one could imagine, I was glad I got to the hospital in time, despite my shower at home.

Before the anesthesia kicked in prior to surgery, my last words to the surgeon were, "Doc, this cowboy can't do the two-step with only one leg." But I knew I was in good hands.

My gifted doctor is the reason I am still here today to write my story. Everyone at the VA Hospital was wonderful and compassionate. I owe them my life.

Sometimes I speculate about my medical problems. Were they brought on by the time I spent in Vietnam or did Vietnam just exacerbate them? I don't know the answer, completely, but my doctor did tell me my knee problem may have been due to the injuries I sustained when I was shot down in Vietnam, and it remained dormant for many years.

In the years following the aneurysm surgery, I had two heart attacks and had to have a stint placed internally.

What I am certain of is that although my tour of duty and activities in combat did not kill me, they certainly physically affected my heart.

They also emotionally scarred my soul.

Chapter 8: The Legacy of War

No one returns from war unchanged. No one.

If you survived, it doesn't matter if you served behind a desk or in combat, if you peeled potatoes, repaired aircraft, commanded a unit, or served as company clerk. You are forever different from the person you were before the war. And you are not the only one changed. Your family is also affected.

Obituaries in the newspaper usually list a surviving member of the family who served in the military and in war. There is pride in the service of a family member.

I often think about what I would have become had I not been a soldier.

Would I have been the man I am now, offering assistance to others, supporting my family? Or would I have become a deadbeat? Would I have become a police officer upholding the law, or would I be running from the law? One thing I do know, however, is that I am awfully proud of having been in the military. Though long discharged from the service, I still consider myself a military man.

My regret is not reaching the twenty or twenty-five-year milestone of working for Social Security Administration (SSA) due to an overlapping series of health problems—issues with my heart and with PTSD. I believe both health concerns are related to my tour of duty in Vietnam, either directly or indirectly. As a result, I was designated as unemployable by Veterans Administration and could not achieve full retirement benefits from SSA because I was there seventeen-and-a-half years, not long enough for their requirements. My financial plans may have changed, but I am thankful to receive full disability benefits. How I wanted to achieve twenty-five years!

It wasn't meant to be.

But I found a new purpose after I left SSA, one that helps both other veterans and me in many ways. Despite the fact I play many roles in my life, the predominant one is my identity as a soldier and veteran.

* * *

When I think about Vietnam, which is just about every day, I am amazed that I mustered the backbone not to turn to drugs, as many GIs did. I guess it was due to my father's influence on me. He taught me that for every action I would take in my life, there would be a reaction. It is a basic law of physics and human life, I think. But in war, you see and hear things you would rather have never had to witness. As I said, war changes you.

When I first arrived in Vietnam, I looked forward to making new friends. As time went on, I wasn't so eager to do that. Too many of them had become casualties, and losing them in so violent a manner, their bodies mangled, their faces sometimes destroyed, took its toll on me. It was just too painful, and to this day I often feel guilty they died and I lived while often being in the background servicing gunships, and not always participating in battle. So when I volunteered to be a door gunner to replace the crew chiefs and other gunners who had died or were severely wounded, I did so with a spirit of revenge for the enemy. My kill ratio was very good. I still carry with me the sights and sounds and smells of combat, and the whoop-whoop of the chopper blades. Today, whenever a low-flying helicopter is overhead, it brings me back to the skies over Vietnam.

One of the reasons I turned down the Army's generous bonus to spend another tour of duty "in country" (as being in Vietnam was called), was because of my near blood-lust. I did not want to become a monster.

It isn't easy to put Vietnam behind me. I think it will always walk beside me. I am constantly learning to live with the war as the best experience of my life, and also as the worst experience I endured. It was the best because I became a man during my tour of duty, and have lived, ever since, as a proud veteran who served his country when called. It was the worst experience, because I had to do things I would rather not have done and I saw things no one should have seen. It left me scarred, though mostly still functioning well. I was no different from other returning soldiers of previous wars.

Sometimes I wonder if my failed marriages were due to my PTSD. It could not have been easy for someone to live with my moods and depression, my anger, fear, and nightmares. My third wife told me she would not ever understand me. I responded, "Please don't try to figure me out. You will never succeed. I can't figure myself out; what makes you think you will be able to?"

* * *

I remember the flights home from Vietnam in 1971. Travelling from Seattle back to McAllen, in full uniform, not one person on any flight welcomed me home. Not one. *That* was definitely different from the way GIs from other wars were received at home.

Although news crews came to Vietnam, and one of them accompanied my unit on a mission, I later learned that almost all of the news back home about Vietnam was negative. Public opposition to the war grew into the anti-war movement.

I truly believe biased, distorted "reporting" was presented to Americans at home. As a result, an exaggerated, stereotyped image of the Vietnam veteran seared itself into the consciousness of Americans. We were viewed as drug-addicted, baby-killing, village-burning, driftless young men who refused direct orders and inflated body counts. Somehow, through the media, we became the bad guys. Inaccurately, we soldiers were blamed for that lost war.

The Vietnam War was lost in Washington D.C., not Vietnam.

In the years immediately after the war and through the end of the 1970s, Vietnam vets often faced discrimination in the open job market, and there was reluctance to publish their stories anywhere. We veterans felt like we were considered socially deviant, violent delinquents. Even the American Legion denied us membership, at least initially, as though American blood spilled in Vietnam was not as worthy as American blood spilled in Europe or Korea.

Hollywood also did its share to demonize Vietnam veterans. Many films portrayed vets as mentally-impaired, drug- or alcohol-addicted killing machines with no hope for a normal life afterwards.

I am a testament against the inaccuracies and biased agenda of the media. So are the vast majority of Vietnam veterans who have raised families and are living productive and fulfilling lives. I am not free of post-war issues and I don't think I will ever fully escape them, but I can handle them now. The extent to which the media and Hollywood vilified Vietnam veterans may have made it more difficult for me and others to integrate back into American society. Maybe that is why we band together and wear our decorations and build our lives around our veteran identity. I can't prove the media contributed to veterans' problems, but I feel it; and it does mean I do not trust those who report the news to we Americans.

* * *

My job in Albuquerque with Social Security put me on a path to a certain level of financial constancy, which was a comfortable place for me to be. Vietnam was long in the past, and my life was stable. Then came the wars in Afghanistan and Iraq, conflicts brought on by the terrorist attacks on the United States in 2001. Like Vietnam, they were guerilla wars.

Never in my wildest dreams did I think my career with SSA would be cut short after less than eighteen years, and not the twenty-five years I hoped to achieve. It started with mornings being somehow different from how they had been. I woke up extremely anxious and agitated. Sometimes the opposite happened: numbing depression would take over. My insides felt like a bowl of Jell-O being shaken. I started missing work over and over, and drained all the leave I had. My supervisor, Betty, had no choice but to place me on restricted leave status. She was patient and caring, and as my descent into full-blown PTSD progressed, my respect for her increased.

One morning, it was so bad I called in sick to work again. I am sure everyone was tired of my being out so often. Not knowing what else to do, I went outside, turned on the hose, and proceeded to water the plants. Within a moment, a beautiful, iridescent hummingbird swooped down to take a drink from the hose. I watched as it hovered before me, its beating wings making a blur. It was not afraid of me.

That beautiful, simple little bird brought me to my knees in peace. Sometimes, I wonder if the bird was a message from God...a message telling me everything will be OK. My internal shaking subsided, and I was able to sit outside for a few hours, more relaxed and grateful. I knew what I had to do.

Within a few days, I headed for the VA Hospital in Albuquerque. That hummingbird told me what I needed.

I went directly to the offices of the Beacon Group and begged them to let me see a psychiatrist or any available therapist. They agreed, and that day, they started me on a path of recovery with the right medications to help me control my anxiety and mood swings. I was also developing a problem with alcohol and wanted to address it early. They connected me with the SUD (Substance Use Disorder) Program where I became involved with group therapy, even though I felt I did not have a substance abuse problem. My therapy group included veterans who had various issues such as extreme PTSD, alcoholism, and drug addiction. At first, I fought the idea of going into a group setting because of my desire for privacy. Revealing my trials and tribulations to a bunch of strangers did not appeal to me. After meeting with the SUD staff, I came to realize that the group really could be a benefit for me, and me for them. Our collective experiences and ways of coping would benefit all of us. I wanted to get out of this spiral, and remembered my Dad advising me that if I wanted anything in life, I must work for it. Well, I wanted to get past this PTSD crisis, and I would do whatever I needed to do to get better.

Image of Hummingbird

Artist Laureen Kent drew and painted this watercolor image of a hummingbird, which reminded Ernest of the sense of peace he felt when the tiny bird visited him as he watered his garden.

Photo: Courtesy Ernest Garcia

I learned that the news coming out of Iraq and Afghanistan, the images of flag-draped coffins being removed from the bellies of airplanes, and the sounds of the Mideast war triggered my PTSD. Apparently, it had been dormant for a long time and came out only in small ways for many years. It erupted with a vengeance because of these new wars. I may as well have been back in Vietnam.

When I completed the SUD program, I was assigned to a counselor for one-on-one therapy. Sonya, my therapist, guided me through tough times and challenged me. She turned me around, and helped me learn how to think in a helpful, rather than harmful way.

Looking back, my opinion of the war and whether it was vital to American interests does not really matter. I am certain, however, it was a war the military was not permitted to win. On many occasions, when I was overhead in a helicopter and fulfilling my role as door gunner, we were shot at from the ground below. We had to radio headquarters to ask if we could fire back. Usually we did not know why we were prohibited from fighting back. Were there special forces on the ground or reconnaissance patrols? We did not know. Often we questioned why we were even sent to a site if we were not permitted to engage in combat with those who were trying to kill us!

It was a confusing war that confounded aerial search and destroy units. We thought we were supposed to fight to win.

* * *

Statistics are grim. When you look at the number of both soldiers and civilians killed, wounded, or missing in Vietnam on both sides, about 1,300,000 died.

There are many sources for statistics about the casualties in Vietnam, and there are usually differences among them.

Below are the American military casualty counts for Vietnam. Taken from the National Archives, these numbers are considered information only, and are not official statistics.

Category of Death	Number
ACCIDENT	9,107
DECLARED DEAD	1,201
DIED OF WOUNDS	5,299
HOMICIDE	236
ILLNESS	938
KILLED IN ACTION	40,934
PRESUMED DEAD (BODY REMAINS RECOVERED)	32
PRESUMED DEAD (BODY REMAINS NOT RECOVERED)	91
SELF-INFLICTED	382
Total	58,220

Branch of Service	Number
AIR FORCE	2586
ARMY	38,224
COAST GUARD	7
MARINE CORPS	14,844
NAVY	2,559
Total	58,220

The U.S. Department of Veterans Affairs provides the following numbers regarding the US military and its engagement in Vietnam, 1964-1975:

Category	Number
MILITARY DEPLOYED TO SOUTHEAST ASIA	3,403,000
BATTLE DEATHS	47, 434
OTHER DEATHS (IN THEATER OF WAR)	10,786
OTHER DEATHS IN SERVICE (NON-THEATER OF WAR)	32,000
NON-MORTAL WOUNDINGS	153,303

Numbers do not tell the whole story, however. The soldiers in the following list are those I knew, either closely as co-workers, or casually. They are the ones who never came home. Their faces are still quite clear to me...all forty of them.

KIA: Killed in Action; **MIA**: Missing in Action; **POW:** Prisoner of War

Name	Rank	Status	Date
Armentrout, Raymond L.	Sergeant	KIA	3/2/1971
Barger, Kenneth Allen	Chief Warrant Officer	KIA	2/11/1971
Beckwith III, Harry M.	Sergeant	KIA	3/24/1971
Berdahl, David D.	Private First Class	MIA, body never recovered	1/20/1972
Brooks, Jackie Ray	Private First Class	KIA	9/22/1970
Carroll, Raymond Frank	Private First Class	KIA	2/11/1971
Carter, Paul D.	Captain	KIA	5/5/1971
Coker, David L.	Captain	KIA	3/24/1971
Denmark, Robert Lee	Specialist 4	KIA	12/31/1971
Dunaway, Robert Leon	Specialist 4	KIA	8/22/1970
Easton, David Everett	Specialist 5	KIA	3/11/1971
Edwards, Harry J.	Specialist 4	MIA, body never recovered	1/20/1972
Figueroa, Fernando	Specialist 5	MIA, body never recovered	1/24/1972
Foy, Jerry	Warrant Officer 1	KIA	2/27/1971
Gronberg Jr., Martin W.	Captain	KIA	9/4/1971
Hanson, Steven R.	Warrant Officer 1	KIA	9/4/1971
Hiscock, Steven Mayo	Chief Warrant Officer	KIA	2/23/1971
Holian, Gary L.	SP/4	KIA	8/12/1971
Hubrins, Eddie Barry	Sergeant	KIA	12/15/1971
Hunter, John Clark	1st. Lieutenant	KIA	2/20/1971
Jones, Neil Wade	Specialist 4	KIA	12/31/1971
Kelly, Eric S.	Specialist 5	KIA	8/12/1971
Kelly, Lawrence L.	1st. Lieutenant	KIA	8/12/1971
Lockhart, John Thomas	Specialist 5	KIA	3/11/1971
McCoy, Larry	PFC - E3	KIA	8/12/1971
Moran, Walter C.B.	Specialist 4	MIA, body never recovered	1/23/1971
Nacca Jr., Carl	Warrant Officer	KIA	2/20/1971

Name	Rank	Status	Date
Neal, William Edward	Specialist 4	KIA	3/24/1971
Nelson, Robert	Specialist 5	KIA	8/12/1971
Paul, James L.	Warrant Officer 1	KIA	2/5/1971
Peck, Steven Russell	Warrant Officer	KIA	3/15/1971
Scharnberg, Ronald O .	Major	KIA	3/17/1971
Schlutter, William David	1st. Lieutenant	KIA	3/17/1971
Strickland, Gail L.	SP/4	KIA	8/12/1971
Sutton, Bryan James	Lieutenant Colonel	KIA	3/17/1971
Thompson, John	1st. Lieutenant	KIA	8/12/1971
Walerzak, William T.	Specialist 4	KIA	2/23/1971
Walters, Robert Daniel	Private First Class	KIA	3/24/1971
Wood, Carl Mitchell	Warrant Officer	KIA	2/5/1971
Wright, James	Sergeant	KIA	8/12/1971

POW/MIA Flag

This image depicts the flag of the National League of Families of American Prisoners and Missing in Southeast Asia. It symbolizes our nation's commitment to bringing closure to families who service members were unaccounted for and considered either prisoners or missing. On a single flag pole, it is flown beneath the American flag.

Image is in the public domain

An Aerial View of the Vietnam Veterans Memorial Wall

Designed by American architect Maya Lin, the Vietnam Memorial in Washington D.C. consists of three components: 1) The wall bearing the names of U.S. Armed Services members KIA (Killed in Action), MIA (Missing in Action), or POW (Prisoners of War) who died; 2) a statue titled "The Three Servicemen" by Frederick Hart, which purposefully depicts the soldiers as African American, European American, and Hispanic American, and 3) The Vietnam Women's Memorial designed by Glenna Goodacre. It depicts uniformed women assisting a wounded soldier. Most servicewomen in the war were nurses.

Public Domain, https://commons.wikimedia.org/w/index.php?curid=78216

Close-up of Names on the Wall

Names on the wall are listed alphabetically by year of death from 1959 through 1975, although it was later determined there were some deaths as early as 1957. Originally, the wall listed 58,191 servicemembers when it was completed in 1983, but as of May 2017, 58,318 names are engraved on it, including eight women. About 1,200 names are of those service members listed as missing (MIAs, POWs, and others).

The Three Servicemen Statue

This bronze sculpture by Frederick Hart portrays three young American soldiers. They were purposely designed to depict the predominant ethnic groups who served in Vietnam. On the left, Latino; in the center, European, and on the right, African American.

R. Wellen Photography/Shutterstock.com

Vietnam Women's War Memorial

This bronze statue, designed by Glenna Goodacre, is dedicated to the uniformed women who served in the Vietnam War and honors their service. Most of them were nurses and the statue shows them aiding a wounded soldier.

LeeAnn White/Shutterstock.com

When I look at the names of all the war dead, I sometimes think about today's violence in the United States, with its high homicide rate compared to the rest of the world. If the people who commit murders here at home had to endure what combat veterans did, having to kill the enemy, would murderers at home think hard before pulling the trigger? Would they so easily slaughter their neighbors, and even little children?

Our prisons are full of those who have killed. As someone whose job it was to return fire against an enemy firing at me, I hope people here at home will think twice before taking a human life.

Although I am proud to be a veteran and am deeply involved with helping other military survivors of the war, sometimes I do still feel anxious or depressed. When that happens, I seek help.

I wish those who might kill here at home would do the same.

Chapter 9: Giving Back - Helping Veterans

There was a draft in place during the years I served in Vietnam. I chose to enlist, rather than be drafted. The draft ended in 1973, and now the U.S. has a volunteer military. I believe the concept of a volunteer military is great, but I also believe it lowers the bar for our country being a superpower with unprecedented military might. Technology is great in fighting a war, but there are times when sheer numbers of military personnel are needed. Perhaps mandatory service of some kind should be required.

If a draft were set in place, then before a major military conflict arises, we will have a reservoir of trained personnel all focused on the same objectives. There wouldn't be an "us" vs. "them" mentality of those who serve compared to those who do not serve their country. I chose to enlist rather than be drafted, because enlisted personnel had some say in the jobs they might wish to pursue within the service. When a person decided not to enlist, but waited to be drafted, then the enlistee could be assigned to a Military Occupational Specialty that had no alignment with his talents or interests.

Enlisting solved that problem for me. I wanted to be an avionics specialist, and became one in the Army.

I think more people should enlist in a branch of the military and spend part of their lives in service to their country. It will help bind us together better than today's situation of "some people defend our freedoms" vs. "let someone else defend our freedoms."

That said, I now help veterans. This work benefits me as well as those I work with on a daily basis. Their healing is my healing.

Live Theater

One of the most satisfying activities I have been involved with is the *Telling, Albuquerque* project.

I was contacted by Circe Olson Woessner, PhD., Director of the Museum of the American Military Family in Tijeras, New Mexico, to consider auditioning for a part in the performance of *Telling, Albuquerque*. In turn, I was interviewed via phone by Max Rayneard, the producer and senior writer, and selected as a cast member.

It was such an eye-opener, coming from being a veteran to a performer, live, on stage! The production staff constantly encouraged those of us in the cast, and we participated in countless rehearsals. I realized that my training in the Dale Carnegie methods really helped me on stage.

The performance allowed me to tell my story and exposed the audience to the hidden and not-so-hidden pains of being a war veteran, in my case. Other members of the cast were military spouses, military "brats" (children of military personnel), officers, transgender service members, and others. Everyone—not just those deployed to a conflict zone—is affected by war and military life. *Telling, Albuquerque* made that clear.

The Telling Project

Ernest honors the dead, symbolized by the pair of empty boots in the *Telling, Albuquerque* live performance.

Photo provided by Ernest Garcia, courtesy of Max Rayneard

The Telling Project

Members of the cast of *Telling, Albuquerque* represent various groups of people associated with the military. Cast members, from the left: Allen Whitt (Navy veteran), Mary Kay Chapman (Air Force veteran), Ernest Garcia (Army veteran), Jacqueline Murray Long (spouse of veteran), and Iain Woessner (child of veteran).

Producer and Senior Writer: Max Rayneard
Writers: Max and Caroline Le Blanc

Photo courtesy Circe Olson Woessner, MAMF (Museum of the American Military Family)

Museum of the American Military Family

I have been on the advisory board of the Museum of the American Military Family for over three years. Located in Tijeras, New Mexico, just east of Albuquerque, the museum's mission is to educate the public and honor America's military members and their families by providing insightful exhibits, workshops, and discussion groups.

The board is small, independent, and totally volunteer. According to founder and director, Dr. Circe Olson Woesnner, the museum collects and preserves stories, photographs, artifacts, and documents from generations of American military families. It is about the mothers and fathers, sons and daughters, spouses and partners, and others who support members of our armed forces.

The museum is a place for people with a connection to someone in the military to come together as a community. It is a repository of their stories, and a place to understand the impact of military service on the families—both those who serve while wearing a uniform, and those who serve without a uniform.

Some of the programs the Museum has been involved in are:

Telling, Albuquerque [a live performance]

Film Series: *Brown Babies, Brats, Service: When Women Come Marching Home, We Served Too, Brothers at War, Stray Dog*, others

Operation Footlocker

Standing Down Literature discussion group-(National Endowment Humanities/Great Books.org)

The Postcard Project

Workshops: Resiliency-Veterans Wellness Conference, Brats 101; Fatigues to Flags: Transformational Paper Making (March 2017) Created Anthology and will host reading/discussion groups (February-March 2017)

4 Voices of the 4th

Vietnam: A Tale of Two Wars (April 30, 2017) War Child: Lessons Learned from Growing Up in War (Anthology to be published 11/2017)

SHOUT: Sharing our Truths (Anthology to be published 10/2017)

Veteran Motorcyclist Oral History Project (Fall 2017)

Museum of the American Military Family (MAMF)

The sign above the storefront museum welcomes military family members and all visitors. The museum is located in Tejeras, New Mexico.

Photo courtesy Circe Olson Woessner, MAMF

Museum of the American Military Family (MAMF)

Inside the museum are many exhibits depicting life in the service for both the servicemembers and their families.

Photo courtesy Circe Olson Woessner, MAMF

Membership in Veterans Organization

Ever since DAV (Disabled American Veterans) gave me a donation of $500 after my home was destroyed in the Wichita Falls tornado, I have been involved in organizations that assist veterans.

When I got back on my feet and returned to McAllen, I joined the VFW (Veterans of Foreign Wars) and participated in hundreds of community service projects.

For one major project, I was chairman of the Vietnam Veterans Reunion in South Texas, and an officer in the formation of the Last Patrol organization that honors the sacrifices of South Texas military heroes.

Since we could not afford to bring the travelling wall of the names of the Vietnam War dead to McAllen, we built our own memorial out of plywood, painted it black, and hand-stenciled the names of fallen Vietnam service members from each city in South Texas. We entered our wall as a parade float in the Memorial Day Parade, 1988. We were awarded the 1st place trophy, which was presented to the VFW (Veterans of Foreign Wars) Post 8788 in McAllen. I was a member for twelve years before moving to Albuquerque.

After some time in Albuquerque, I moved to nearby Rio Rancho and joined a VFW Post. I met a wonderful Post Commander, Ty Teel, and his wife, Tessa. We became good friends, and before I knew what happened, he encouraged me to run for Junior Vice Commander. My tenure in that position was both successful and satisfying. We had so many interesting and meaningful projects like the flag retirement ceremonies and Memorial and Veterans day parades and celebrations. As a result, our post was honored by VFW National Headquarters with that National Community Service Award.

I worked my way through the chairmanships to become Post Commander, which paved the way for me to become District 2

Senior vice Commander, and finally, District Commander, overseeing nine posts in the district.

The Wall in South Texas

A smaller version of "The Wall" honors the 146 South Texas service members who died in Vietnam or were missing in action. The locations represented are: Mission, Edinburg, Brownsville, Harlingen, McAllen, San Benito, and Weslaco. From the left: Rick Walters, Ruben Guerra, and Ernest Garcia honor those served and gave their lives.

Photo credit Kathleen Holton, courtesy of Ernest Garcia
McAllen[Texas] Town Crier.

As I write this book, I hold the position of 2nd Jr. Vice Commander of Disabled American Veterans, Chapter 5, and expect to move up through the chairs, if all goes well. My chapter has been heavily involved in community activities, one of which is visiting and honoring veterans in senior living facilities. I enjoy doing this, and the veterans, some of whom served in World War II, are very moved by the fact we have not forgotten them.

Honoring Veterans at the Pamilla Senior Living

Ernest (second from left) frequently visits veterans around New Mexico. Here he is with some other veterans who visited the Palmilla Senior Home in Albuquerque. His group conducted a program to honor veterans and then adjourned outside to take this photo. Ernest is second from left.

Photo courtesy Ernest Garcia

Some other activities are marching in parades, and partnering with the Boy Scouts of American to properly retire American flags that are no longer fit for active use.

* * *

There are many organizations for veterans, and I am currently an active participant in the following ones:

1) VFW: Past Post Jr. Vice Cmdr., Past post Cmdr.; Past District Sr. Vice Cmdr.; Past District Cmdr.; Life Member

2) DAV 2nd Jr. Vice Cmdr. Chapter 5; life member

3) Life member of the National Order of Trench Rats, also a part of the DAV.

4) American Legion member post 69

5) Elks Lodge past Veterans Liaison

6) Loyal Order of Moose

7) Rio Rancho Veterans Coffee Group member

8) Fraternal Order of Eagles

Chapter 10: Honors, Accolades, and Awards

It was always my goal to do the best job I could do, whether it was in civilian or military life. In many instances I succeeded, and I have received many honorary citations, trophies, and awards.

Yet, my greatest satisfaction comes from helping veterans by honoring them, helping them secure the benefits they've earned, participating in ceremonies designed to recognize them, and just being one, myself.

There is a popular saying, "Do what you love, the money will come" and I often think about it. Although I have not become rich being a veteran and helping other veterans, I have certainly been acknowledged for my contributions in life. I'd like to share some of them with you on the following pages.

Sometimes, I am still surprised a poor kid from the barrio in South Texas has accomplished so much.

I hope my story has been an inspiration for today's kids who come from a comparable situation.

Insurance Awards

Ernest received several awards while working as an insurance agent for Western & Southern Life Insurance, in the Harlingen, Texas District. From the Left: Sales Representative of the month, awarded in 1995; The large center trophy was awarded in 1994 for "Rookie of the Year" and on the right is another trophy awarded in 1992.

Photo courtesy Ernest Garcia

Ernest's Medals and Insignia

Ernest has many medals and insignia.

<u>Top, left to right</u>: Air Medal (partially visible), Vietnam Campaign Medal, The Bronze Star, National Defense Service Medal, Republic of Vietnam Service Medal with 2 Campaign Service Stars

<u>Bottom</u>: left to right: Flight Wings, Door Gunner Insignia, the Calvary Crossed swords, 2nd National Defense Service Medal (partially visible)

<u>Not shown</u>: Commendation Medal, Expert Marksmanship Medal, U.S. Army Challenge Coin

Photo courtesy Ernest Garcia

Military Order of the Purple Heart

This plaque acknowledges Ernest for his work in bringing the Vietnam Traveling Wall to Rio Rancho, New Mexico.

Photo courtesy Ernest Garcia

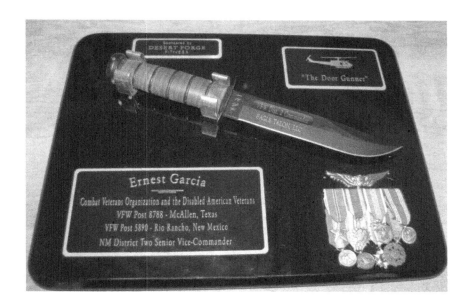

Eagle Talon Award

Ernest Received a Lifetime Hero's Achievement Award.

This prestigious acknowledgement is given to noted veterans who continue working in service to other veterans and the community at large. The recipient has to be a combat veteran. Eagle Talon LLC is a non-profit organization led by Mr. Clarence Gallegos.

Photo courtesy Ernest Garcia

Medal Close-up

Top: Crew member Flight Wings, flying as a Door gunner

Top row, from the left: Bronze Star, Air Medal, Army Commendation Medal, and National Defense Service Medal

Bottom row, from the left: National Defense Service Medal (duplicated in error), Viet Nam Campaign Medal, Vietnam Service Medal, Republic of Vietnam Cross of Gallantry, issued by the President of South Vietnam to those who also served into the Cambodian Excursion and into Laos.

Photo courtesy Ernest Garcia.

Chapter 11: Tomorrow

As I write this book, a new member of my family brings me love and peace, just as the hummingbird did the day I realized I needed help with PTSD.

I am talking about my dog, Pepito, a stray who has become part of my life. I found him in the South Valley of Albuquerque. He was wandering alone and confused in a heavily congested area. My wife and I fell in love with him instantly.

Pepito

Pepito offers Ernest and his wife love,
peace and companionship every day.

Photo courtesy Ernest Garcia

With Pepito at my side, I have just started a new business titled Ernest Garcia: Social Security Benefits Consultant, LLC. With seventeen years of service as an employee of Social Security Administration, I now use the skills I mastered in my job there to help others, mostly veterans, secure the benefits they deserve.

I manage their cases through all the steps necessary for being approved for disability benefits. This process sometimes includes Congressional intervention. Along the way, I have come to appreciate New Mexico's Congressional and Senate elected officials who support efforts to ensure veterans who have been wrongfully denied disability benefits are ultimately granted them. When working with people who use my services, I help identify their needs and offer them guidance about how to protect themselves and their families from many of life's uncertainties. That's where my former job as a life insurance agent really comes into play. I make clients aware of solutions to their issues, identify the resources they require, and help them secure whatever they need. In the end, they retain the power to make the choices necessary for both themselves, their spouses, and children.

I tell each veteran, and anyone, really, to follow his dream and tell his or her story. It is OK to talk about struggles, to let your emotions show. They will be proud they did. People need to hear the stories of veterans in any form or fashion.

There is no reason to hold back!

My many memberships in the organizations mentioned in the previous chapter give me the opportunity to meet veterans in need of assistance. The most prominent support systems have come from Eagle Talon LLC, headed by Clarence Gallegos and Jason Griego Krypteia LLC. Together we have opened many doors for veterans in need of the services of DVR (Division of Vocational Rehab) in Rio Rancho and SBA (Small Business Administration).

With all the insights and experience I have gained over the years in all the jobs I have held, it would be a terrible thing to just tuck that knowledge away and never use it again.

Why waste it?

Acknowledgements

No one goes through life completely alone, and I have been blessed to enjoy the friendship, guidance, and assistance of some very special people.

My wife, Annabelle

 Annabelle supported me through this endeavor of writing my memoir, and helped in many ways, from typing and preparing documents to feeding me well, to always being there for me. I have known her for over twenty years as she pursued a career working for the City of Albuquerque and then as the municipal clerk of the Village of Los Ranchos. During her twenty-seven-year tenure, she reported to eight mayors. In 2005 she received the Municipal Clerk of the Year award in New Mexico. Annabelle is my loving, caring, and faithful companion in life.

Ismael Gonzalez, Sr.—my grandfather

Ismael Gonzalez, Sr., my mother's father, left a legacy of being a businessman in McAllen, Texas, with his own grocery store.

Mr. Danny Aragon

Danny is a generous spirit with great compassion. He and his wife opened up a world of genuine friendship to me. They have invited me into their home and to celebrate various feast days with them at Sandia Pueblo. Danny has served as Lieutenant War Chief, War Chief, and Councilman for his pueblo. His friendship to me and his devotion to his people are immeasurable.

Mr. Paul Bentley

Paul was one of the arresting detectives who handled assassin Lee Harvey Oswald. Later he headed the security management team at a Dallas bank. Paul took me under his wing and exposed me to people and associations involved in the security business. I learned much from him and knew I disappointed him when I left the bank. He helped me develop both skills and confidence. I deeply appreciate and respect him.

Mr. Luis Perez

Luis was my manager and mentor at the insurance company. He taught me a lot and believed in me. I am grateful for his guidance and friendship.

Manuel (Manny) Rodriguez

Manny is a true, close friend and a wonderful, compassionate Vietnam veteran.

Fred Ortiz

Fred is the Past VFW National Service Officer who has always been by our side through sickness and health. Fred fought the VA and the OPM (Office of Personnel Management) to obtain the benefits I earned, gaining my 100% disability rating and unemployable status.

Sal Soto

Sal is a friend and confidant, rather like the skull "Wilson" I kept on the dashboard of my truck for a while.

Circe Olson Woessner, PhD. and Paul Zolbrod

As Director of the Museum of the American Military Family and writer-in-residence, respectively, Circe and Paul helped me kick-start creation of this book. Circe invited me to become a member of the museum and a website contributor.

Patricia Walkow, Author and Editor

Patricia Walkow, award-winning author of *The War Within, the Story of Josef*, took the time to help me fulfill a dream by helping me finish this book and prepare it for publication, thereby telling my story.

Clarence Gallegos, President of Eagle Talon

Clarence's passion and compassion toward veterans is something I admire tremendously. He and I have worked tirelessly to ensure veterans receive the benefits and assistance they earned from both Social Security and Veterans Affairs. He firmly believes in the following unattributed definition of a veteran:

A veteran, whether active duty, retired, National Guard, or Reserve, is someone who, at one point in his or her life, wrote a blank check, made "payable to the United States of America for the amount of up to and including my life."

Valerie Espinoza

Valerie Espinoza, New Mexico Commissioner District 3 Chair, Public Regulation Commission, invited Clarence Gallegos, Victor Delgado, Cindy Delgado, and Ernest Garcia on her SFCTV16 (Santa Fe Community College) television program, *One on One*.

The exposure helped us reach out to New Mexico veterans as well as publicize the American Museum of the Military Family.

Bryan Farmer

Bryan was my business advisor at the Small Business Development Center in Rio Rancho, New Mexico. He was instrumental in helping me fund and set up my business.

Robert Brown

Robert Brown is a special breed of man whose generosity and compassion has helped Disabled American Veterans (DAV) Chapter 5 in Rio Rancho achieve its goals.

Heroes in my Family

Felix Garcia, Sr.—my father
Dad is still my hero. He served as a Private in the U.S. Army in World War II and received the WWII Victory Medal and The Honorable Service Lapel Button. We lost him on December 6, 1979. Rest in peace, Dad.

Uncle Faustino Garcia, Sr.

Uncle Faustino was my father's brother. He was a World War II veteran of the U.S. Army 8th Air Force. He died at 96 years old.

Uncle Ismael Gonzalez, Jr.

Uncle Ismael, my mother's brother, is a U.S. Army veteran of the Korean War. In the 1960s he was an activist with the United Farm Workers, led by Cesar Chavez. He often donated food from his grocery story to farm workers. He died in October 2007 at the age of 77.

Uncle Gilberto Gonzalez

Uncle Gilbert served in the U.S. Army as a paratrooper during the Korean War. When he returned home, he helped manage the family business that distributed tamales, El Valle Chorizo Company, in Mission, Texas.

Uncle Anthony Pons, Sr.

Uncle Anthony, my mother's sister's husband, served his country as a member of the U.S. Army Air Corps.

Cousin Faustino Garcia, Jr.

As a member of the U.S. Navy, Faustino served off the coast of Vietnam on the USS Buchanan, a destroyer. His best friend, Joe Ramos, also served as a Helicopter Crew Chief and was killed in action on 9/15/1970. Faustino escorted the remains of his friend back to the U.S. for full military honors burial.

Felix Garcia, Jr.

Felix is my older brother. He served in the U.S. Army with the Army Security Agency, and then with the U.S. Air Force. At Baylor Medical Center in Dallas, Texas, he was a pulmonary technician. He also worked with the Houston Police Department.

Danny Garcia

Danny is my brother and served with the U.S. Air Force, INS (Immigration and Nationalization Service), and Customs. He has worked as a Special Agent for Homeland Security and is now with Department of Veterans Affairs in Washington, D.C. His years of service have been impressive, and I am proud that another Garcia from the barrio has achieved such success. He should write his own book.

Alice Garcia, niece

Alice is the first in the family to graduate from West Point Military Academy. She is the daughter of my brother, Felix.

Jennifer Garcia, niece

Jennifer graduated from West Point Preparatory School and decided to go on active duty right after graduation.

Other family members who served, on my mother's side:

Richard Gonzalez, Sr:

U.S. Marines, probably during the Korean Conflict

Richard Gonzalez Jr.

U.S. Army, around 1976-1978

Steve Kleczk

Six years in the Army Reserves 1152nd Transportation unit in Milwaukee; basic training in Fort Leonard Wood Missouri September of 1982 through 1988

William Hatcher Sr.

U.S. Marines, probably around the Korean Conflict

Thoughts on Pride, Deployment, and Sacrifice

Pride

Pride is a connection between the mind and the heart that controls the never-ending love of American heroes who trusted their upbringing of love of country and flag that helped shape the U.S.A. into what it is today. We gave of ourselves, one vet at a time. That's what keeps us walking tall, and no one can ever take that away from us!

Deployment

Deployment is when reality sets in that you are going to a war zone or a combat theater, not knowing what the future holds for you, much less your family and loved ones. Sitting at the airport with your friends and family as you approach departure, you pretend that you are OK and prepared for the heavy burden you carry into the future. There is no turning back to your childhood, and one says an internal prayer:

Please help me become a man for my country.

Sacrifice

A prayer: Dear God, if you have to take me before my designated time, I hereby give myself to You and my country, with the honor I intended. Please ensure that my loved ones do not suffer without pride, and that they know my fate was for them and my country, equally.

Appendix

Ernest Garcia's Military History

Print   Subscribe   Share/Save

Ernest Phillip Garcia Collection

Biographical Information

Name:
Ernest Phillip Garcia
State of Birth:
MO
Home State:
NM

Gender
Male
Race
Hispanic

War or Conflict
Vietnam War, 1961-1975
Military Status
Veteran
Dates of Service
1969-1972
Entrance into Service
Enlisted
Branch of Service
Army
Unit of Service
1st Aviation Brigade; 9th Infantry Division
Location of Service
Fort Bliss, Texas; Fort Gordon, Georgia; Quang Tri,
Vietnam; Fort Sill, Oklahoma
Battles/Campaigns
Operation Lam Son 719
Highest Rank
Specialist Five
Prisoner of War
No
Service History Note
The veteran served as an avionics specialist and a
helicopter door gunner

Collection Information

Type of Resource:
Audio: CD [1 item] -- Oral history interview
Audio: CD [1 item] -- Oral history interview
Photograph: Digital print [2 items] -- Photographs
Audio: CD [1 item] -- Reference copy
Audio: CD [1 item] -- Reference copy
Interviewer:
Karoline Bota
Contributor:
Lee Courtnage
Contributor Affiliation/Organization:
OASIS of Albuquerque, New Mexico
Collection #:
AFC/2001/001/84224
Subjects:
Garcia, Ernest Phillip
Vietnam War, 1961-1975--Personal Narratives
United States. Army
Cite as:
Ernest Phillip Garcia Collection
(AFC/2001/001/84224), Veterans History Project,
American Folklife Center, Library of Congress

Last Edit: 2016-07-29

XML: MODS Bibliographic Data | METS Object Description

Glossary

TERM	DEFINITION
CO	Commanding Officer
ETS	Expiration of Term of Service
Gook	An ethnic slur that refers to communist soldiers during the Vietnam War
GPS/VOR/LOC	GPS: Global Positioning Systems VOR: Very High Frequency omni-directional radio range LOC: Locator
HF, VHF, UHV	Radio frequencies: High Frequency; Very High Frequency; and Ultra High Frequency
KIA, MIA, POW	KIA: Killed in Action MIA: Missing in Action POW: Prisoner of War
LZ	Landing Zone
mic	microphone
MOS	Military Occupational Specialty
NCO	Non-commissioned officer
NVA	North Vietnamese Army
R and R	Rest and Relaxation - time off
SP/n	Specialist designation; SP/4, SP/5, and so on
Spudder	1. A portable cable-driven drilling oil rig 2. A person who works a spudder rig
USO	United Service Organization, Inc. It provides services, including entertainment, to service members and their families.
Viet Cong, NVA	Viet Cong: Vietnamese enemy of the United States NVA: North Vietnamese Army
Warrant Officer	An officer designated by warrant, rather than by a commission

A Vest Worn with Pride

Ernest Garcia: Son, grandson, brother, nephew, uncle, father, husband, grandfather, avionics specialist, door gunner, and veteran. Insurance salesman, roughneck, Social Security Customer Service representative, veteran's advocate, businessman, Social Security benefits consultant, and author. A man and a soldier.

Photo courtesy Ernest Garcia

For additional copies of

A Cowboy of a Different Kind, visit

http://www.amazon.com
http://www.barnesandnoble.com

86758515R00085

Made in the USA
Columbia, SC
18 January 2018